Graphic Organisers in the Classroom

Effective Use of Mapping Skills

Graphic Organisers in the Classroom

Effective Use of Mapping Skills

Hema Nalini

AUTHORSPRESS

PUBLISHERS OF SCHOLARLY BOOKS

Worldwide Circulation through Authorspress Global Network
First Published 2010
by
Authorspress
E-35/103, Jawahar Park
Laxmi Nagar, Delhi-110 092
e-mail: authorspress@yahoo.com

Graphic Organisers in the Classroom: Effective Use of Mapping Skills
ISBN 978-81-7273-548-7

Printed in India at Tarun Offset, Delhi.

Preface

In the process of thinking, concepts act as the tools of thinking. Concepts help learners to communicate effectively and intelligibly; communication in the classroom involves teachers, students and the lessons or topics. Since concepts are the basic building blocks of communication and main tools of thinking, their organisation in cognitive structures is of great importance.

Graphic Organisers are the most appropriate and serviceable tools for use with students in general and especially for children who are hearing-impaired or speech impaired, for children with autism, mental retardation, Down syndrome, fetal alcohol syndrome, ADHD (Attention Deficit Hyperactivity Disorder), learning disabilities, slow learners and gifted children.

This book discusses the use of such graphic organisers as structured overviews, Venn diagrams, story maps, and character analysis charts to help teachers develop analysis, synthesis and evaluation as critical thinking skills and take little time for preparation.

Concept maps or idea maps or graphic organisers can help students organise information and ideas related to a given topic. Academic success requires various competencies, among them the ability to know and use a variety of tools and techniques to generate and organise information and ideas is of utmost importance. Teachers can make use of these graphic organsers to enhance their teaching and they can encourage learners to device these graphic organisers to enable them comprehend the text and learn better. The goal in using graphic organisers is to organise ideas and examine relationships. This resource book is intended for teachers, parents, learners/students - both typical children in the regular classrooms and special children as it contains practical suggestions for promoting learning. The goal of the technique of concept-mapping is to empower each learner to become self-directed regarding what and how to learn.

V. Hema Nalini

Contents

1

Theories of Learning and their Implications

Learning has always been a focal point and a favourite theme of educational psychologists. Learning is defined as a relatively permanent change in the behaviour of humans as a result of past experiences. Theories of learning explain the mechanism of the learning process. Basically there are three types of theories – connectionist theories, cognitive theories and constructivist theories. The connectionist theories consider learning as a matter of stimulus-response connection; cognitive theorists consider learning as a process of developing insight in the learners. Constructivists emphasise the building of meaning and knowledge that occurs in people's minds when they learn. Constructivism argues that humans generate knowledge and meaning from their experiences.

Constructivism is the label given to a set of theories about learning which fall somewhere between cognitive and humanistic views. If behaviourism treats the organism as a blank slate or box, cognitive theory recognises the importance of the mind in making sense of the material with which it is presented. Nevertheless, it still presupposes that the role of the learner is primarily to assimilate whatever the teacher presents. Social constructivism views each learner as a unique individual with unique needs and backgrounds. It looks at learners as complex and multi-dimensional organisms and suggests that the learner is much more actively involved in a joint enterprise with the teacher of creating ("constructing") new meanings.

Formalisation of the theory of constructivism is generally attributed to Jean Piaget, who articulated mechanisms by which knowledge is internalised by learners. He suggested that through processes of accommodation and assimilation, individuals construct new knowledge from their experiences. According to Piaget, knowledge is not merely transmitted verbally but must be constructed and reconstructed by the learner. Piaget asserted that for a child to know and construct knowledge of the world, the child must act on objects and it is this action which provides knowledge of those objects; the mind organises reality and acts upon it. Piaget mentions three fundamental processes of intellectual growth – *assimilation, accommodation and equilibration.* When individuals assimilate, they incorporate the new experience into an already existing framework or schemes or thought patterns without changing that framework. This may occur when individuals' experiences are aligned with their internal representations of the world, but may also occur as a failure to change a faulty understanding. Accommodation can be understood as the mechanism by which the learner adapts his thought patterns to include incoming new information or new experience; this new experience and reframing one's cognitive structure to hold the new information helps one to learn. Equilibration refers to striking a balance between oneself and the environment. According to Piaget, equilibration is the major factor in explaining why some children advance more quickly in the development of logical intelligence than others. Piaget advocated active discovery learning environment in our schools.

The social learning theory proposed by Bandura (later renamed by Bandura as *social cognitive theory*) emphasises that knowledge is socially constructed and learning occurs observationally through modeling; according to social learning theory, students often learn a great deal simply by observing and imitating other people. Another crucial assumption regarding the nature of the learner concerns the response consequences and source of motivation for learning and rewards and punishments. The highest level of observational learning is achieved by first organising and rehearsing the model behaviour symbolically and then enacting it overtly. Sustaining motivation to learn is strongly dependent on the learner's confidence in his or her potential for learning. Closely related to this is Vygotsky's "zone of proximal development" (Vygotsky 1978) where learners are challenged within close proximity to, yet slightly above, their current level of development. By experiencing the successful completion of challenging tasks, learners gain confidence and motivation to embark on more complex challenges. Vygotsky considers learning as a social and communicative process whereby knowledge is shared and constructed in culturally formed social settings. He believes that social interaction plays a fundamental role in learning and leads to cognitive development.

2

Ausubel's Theory of Meaningful Verbal Learning (Subsumption Theory)

David Ausubel says,

"If I had to reduce all of educational psychology to just one principle, I would say this: The most important single factor influencing learning is what the learner already knows. Ascertain this and teach him accordingly."

He grounded his research on the work of Jean Piaget. Piaget believed that people actively "organise experience".

An advance organiser is a cognitive strategy proposed by Ausubel in his Subsumption Theory, which allows the learner to recall and transfer prior knowledge to the new information being presented. This theory is based on the idea that learning is facilitated, if the learner can find meaning in the new information. If a connection can be made between the new information and previous knowledge, the learning experience will become more meaningful to the learner. Therefore, the new information will be learned. The advance organiser is not a strategy used by the learner, but rather an instructional strategy used by the teacher.

Ausubel's theory is concerned with how individuals learn large amounts of meaningful material from verbal/textual presentations in a school setting (in contrast to theories developed in the context of laboratory experiments). According to Ausubel, learning is based upon the kinds of superordinate, representational, and combinatorial processes that occur during the reception of information. Ausubel contends that "the most important single factor influencing learning is what the learner already knows".

A major instructional mechanism proposed by Ausubel is the use of advance organisers:

> "These organisers are introduced in advance of learning itself, and are also presented at a higher level of abstraction, generality, and inclusiveness; and since the substantive content of a given organizer or series of organizers is selected on the basis of its suitability for explaining, integrating, and interrelating the material they precede, this strategy simultaneously satisfies the substantive as well as the programming criteria for enhancing the organization strength of cognitive structure." (1963 , p. 81).

Ausubel emphasises that advance organisers are different from overviews and summaries which simply emphasize key ideas and are presented at the same level of abstraction and generality as the rest of the material. Organisers act as a subsuming bridge between new learning material and existing related ideas. According to Ausubel, meaningful verbal learning is the acquisition of ideas that are linked to other ideas. It takes place by the interaction between the new concept (the subsumed) and the more inclusive concepts (subsumer) which are already learned. The process of linking the subsumed with the subsumer is known as *subsumption*.

Ausubel's theory has commonalities with Gestalt theories and those that involve schema as a central principle. There are also similarities with Bruner's "spiral learning" model , although Ausubel emphasises that subsumption involves reorganisation of existing cognitive structures not the development of new structures as constructivist theories suggest. Ausubel was apparently influenced by the work of Piaget on cognitive development.

One of the most prominent contribuitions of Ausubel is the concept of 'advance organisers' Advance organisers are introductory ideas or facts or concepts that are general, comprehensive and encompassing in nature. These are fundamental, abstract and inclusive that they can subsume and serve as anchors for firmly holding or linking together all the new information. It serves as the foundation on which the edifice of new cognitive structure is built.

The advance organiser is not a strategy used by the learner, but rather an instructional strategy used by the teacher. In essence, an advance organiser enables learners bridge the gap between prior learning with new learning- the known to the unknown, by including an abstract outline of the new information and a restatement of old knowledge. Theoretically, this will encourage transfer and application of old knowledge, to make the new knowledge more meaningful to the learner.

Ausubel suggests two different types of organisers for two different purposes:

1. Comparative Organisers present a study of the differences between items the student already knows and what they are about to learn.
2. Expository organisers present a basic concept at a very high, abstract level. They can be used in combination also, but it is more likely to be used separately as each has its own separate strength.

Principles of Advance Organisers

1. "Before we can present new material effectively, we must increase the stability and clarity of our student's structures."
2. "The sequence of the curriculum is organised so that each successive learning is carefully related to what has been learned before."
3. Ausubel describes advance organisers as "introductory material presented ahead of the learning task and at a higher level of abstraction and inclusiveness than the learning task itself".

(Direct quote from David Ausubel's Cognitive Learning Theory).

David Ausubel's concept of using advance organisers like little flags or titles and subtitles to help learners organise what they are about to read into a familiar structural pattern.

Ausubel suggests that advance organisers might foster meaningful learning by prompting the student regarding pre-existing superordinate concepts that are already in the student's cognitive structure, and by otherwise providing a context of general concepts into which the student can incorporate progressively differentiated details.

Ausubel claims that by presenting a global representation of the knowledge to be learned, advance organisers might foster "integrative reconciliation" of the subdomains of knowledge - the ability to understand interconnections among the basic concepts in the domain. Thus advance organisers provide the necessary scaffolding for learners to either learn new and unfamiliar material or to integrate new ideas into relatively familiar ideas.

3

Mapping Skills

CHAPTER OVERVIEW

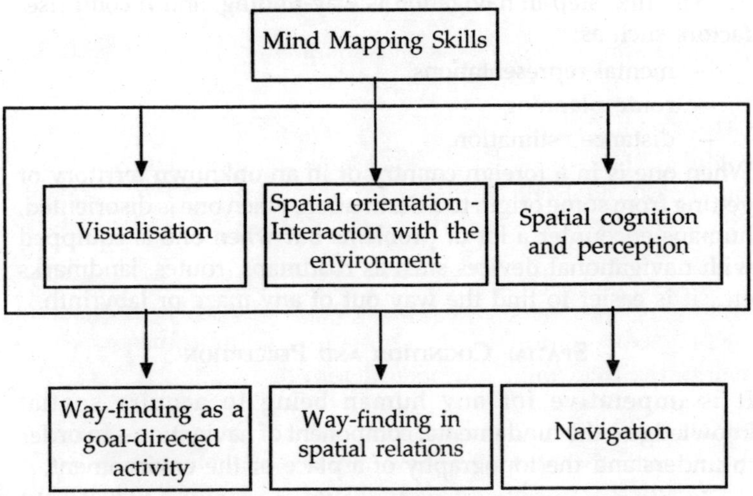

VISUALISATION

Visualisation refers to the process or technique of creating images, diagrams, graphics or pictures or drawing pictures or using illustrations in order to communicate a message. Communicating through visual imagery has been an effective way of sending messages; both abstract and concrete ideas have been effectively communicated for centuries.

Cave paintings, cuneiforms, Chinese/Japanese letters, Egyptian Hieroglyphics, Greek Geometry, Leonardo Da Vinci's technical drawings etc., are classic examples of visualisation techniques. Visualisation has ever-expanding applications in the new millennium in the areas of science, engineering, medicine, social sciences and humanities.

The first step of the process of visualisation is familiarity with the environment otherwise known as spatial orientation. Once a person understands the topography, manoeuvring through the environment becomes easier.

Spatial Orientation

Human beings constantly interact with their environment; crucial and seminal to each individual's interaction is his/ her movement through space. This movement which enables him to understand the environment that he/she lives in is often called navigation.

The first step in navigation is way-finding, and it comprises factors such as:

- mental representations,
- route planning
- distance estimation.

When one is in a foreign country or in an unknown territory or getting from some origin to a destination, when one is disoriented, humans encounter a lot of problems but when one is equipped with navigational devices such as roadmaps, routes, landmarks etc., it is easier to find the way out of any maze or labyrinth.

Spatial Cognition and Perception

It is imperative for any human being to acquire spatial knowledge—the fundamental component of navigation—in order to understand the topography of a place or the environment.

In order to acquire spatial cognition, an individual should develop—perception and cognitive mapping—a thorough comprehension of cognitive aspects of navigation based on which one will be able to make decisions and execute the decision into action.

Way-finding

After the acquisition of spatial cognition, the next step is way-finding. Way-finding is a term borrowed from oceanography. Way-finding was used for voyaging for thousands of years before the invention of European navigational instruments. This involves navigating on the open ocean or unmarked territory without sextant, compass, clock, radio reports, maps, satellite assistance, remote sensors or any other navigational device. Originally sailors in the ocean depended upon stars, the sun, the ocean swells, and other signs of nature for clues to direction and location of a vessel at sea. Modern way-finding refers to the ways in which people, animals and birds or living organisms orient themselves in physical space and navigate from place to place.

People use different strategies of way-finding; but usually they combine the strategies of:

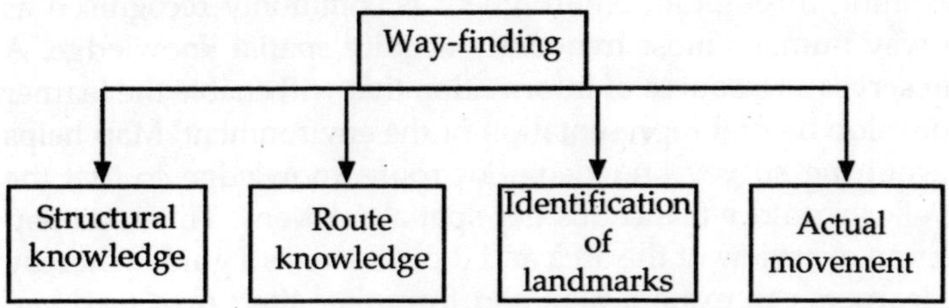

Figure 1: Strategies of Way-finding

- — *Structural or Topographical Survey Knowledge*—the ability to acquire a representation of the spatial environment and the ability to localise within it are essential for successful navigation in unknown environments
- — *Knowledge of different pathways or route knowledge*—enables one to plan routes/make choices and understand where one is going and where one has been; route knowledge is usually gained by personal exploration of a new area, and is ordered sequentially and often structured around features such as landmarks. Paths are static linear structures in an environment; they may be streets, footpaths, pavements, canals, rivers or railway tracks or highways.
- — *The behavioural pattern or movement*—performed by moving along a path is called a route. When moving along a path an individual experiences an organised sequence in which phases follow each other meaningfully in an order. Route following in way-finding also involves recognising an origin and a destination and identifying districts and sequences of features that make up the route.

— *Identification and recognition of Landmarks*—Landmarks act as primary features in the way-finding task; landmarks are visible markers which stand out in a landscape due to its visible form, peculiarity of shape or structure, or because of socio-cultural significance; with the help of sources such as signs, maps, descriptions, and images, human beings begin to explore unknown areas and integrate perceptual stimuli into an internal, consistent representation of the environment.

Way-finding in Spatial Relations

Travelling through an environment is commonly recognised as the way humans most frequently acquire spatial knowledge. A map serves as a source of information that will enable the learner to develop mental representation of the environment. Map helps in acquiring survey knowledge or route knowledge so that the traveller would enhance his/her spatial relations. This roadmap gives an overview of the area and it can serve as a guide whereby the learners can extend, plan and formulate their own learning.

Based on the spatial knowledge acquired from maps, people acquire topographical configurations and layouts. The cognitive element of navigation refers to strategic planning and tactical movement.

Navigation

Navigation tasks are absolutely imperative in any environment that demands movement over large spaces. Navigation is the synthesis of way-finding and motion. It is a combination of both the cognitive element (way-finding), and the kinetic or motoric element (movement techniques).

The traveller gains knowledge and understanding of the space around him or her and forms mental images. These mental images or configurations get internalised and help the learner to understand the space or the environment and permit the direct retrieval of spatial relationships between points without relying on external sources or without reference to the routes connecting them. Navigational strategies include landmarks, routes, regions, and includes comprehension of distances and directions, linkage, connectivity and scale. A further important anchor point in way-finding is the starting point or location. Spatial knowledge must be organised in such a way that it can be used during navigation tasks.

4

Mind Maps

CHAPTER OVERVIEW

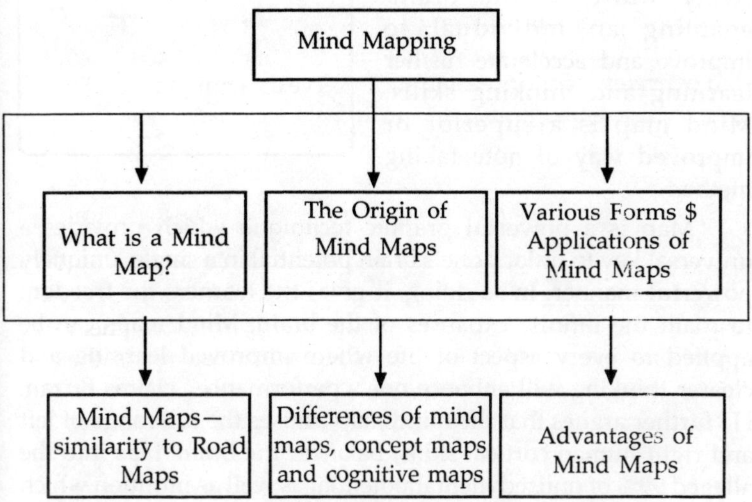

MIND MAPPING

A mind map is a way of organising information and can be defined as a powerful graphic technique for thinking on paper. A mind map is restricted to a learner's reflections on a single topic or single concept. A mind map can be used for keeping notes, or for developing a concept, or for getting an overview of an activity. It is typically an organic multi-colored chart laid out on a large sheet of paper. It contains words and drawings that are connected in various ways.

To put it simply, it refers to the art of converting abstract idea into concrete one. Mind mapping is a concept developed by psychologist Tony Buzan; mind maps can be used in many different situations. They are extremely useful for planning purposes or where the sequencing of events is important. It is both rational and artistic, both logically ordered and spontaneously expressive. Even though, mind mapping is a very old form of presenting information, its usage and application in the contemporary scenario of educational practices has wide scope.

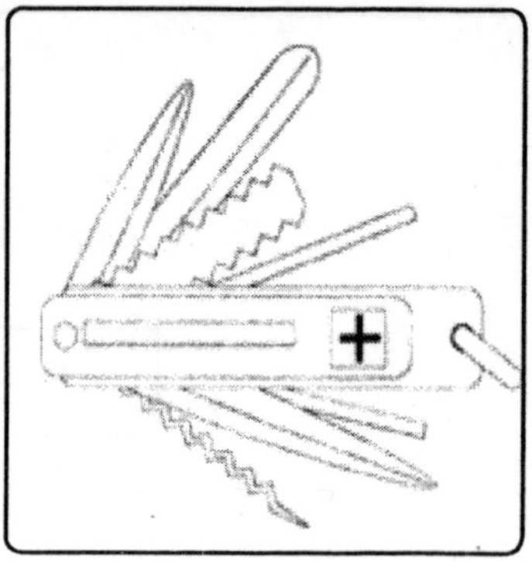

Mind maps act as the 'Swiss Army Knife of the brain' enabling an individual to improve and accelerate his/her learning and thinking skills. Mind map is a superior or improved way of note taking method.

"Map is a powerful graphic technique which provides a universal key to unlock one's brain potential in a single, uniquely powerful manner. In so doing, it gives the learners the freedom to roam the infinite expanses of the brain. Mind maps can be applied to every aspect of life where improved learning and clearer thinking will enhance one's performance" claims Buzan. He further argues that the mind map utilises the full range of left and right human cortical skills, balances the brain, taps into the alleged 99% of unused mental potential as well as intuition which he calls 'superlogic'.

What is Mind Mapping?

Mind mapping refers to the diagrams to represent words, ideas, tasks, or other items linked to and arranged around a central key word or idea. Mind maps are used to generate, visualise, structure, and classify ideas, and as an aid in study, organisation, problem solving, decision making and writing.

The elements of a given mind map are arranged intuitively according to the importance of the concepts and are classified into groupings, branches, or areas, with the goal of representing semantic or other connections between portions of information. Mind maps may also aid recall of existing memories.

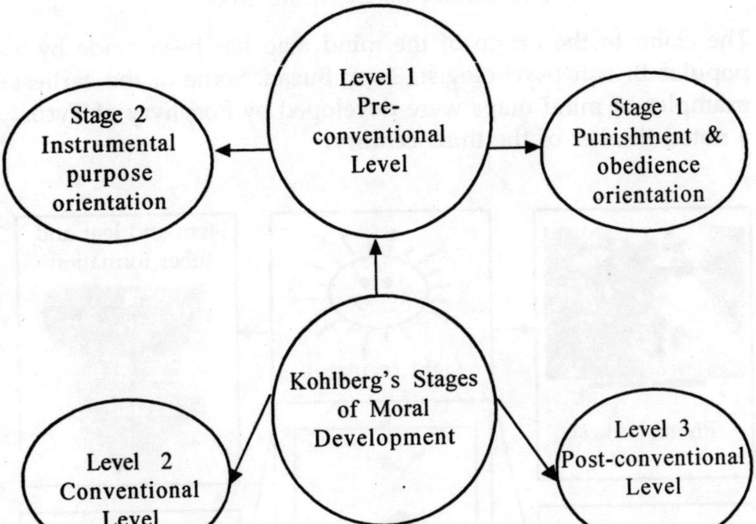

Mind Map on Kohlberg's Stages of Moral Development

A mind map is a diagram used to represent words, ideas, tasks or other items linked to and arranged radially around a central key word or idea; mind maps have been used by educators, engineers and psychologists for:

a) learning,
b) structuring
c) generating ideas
d) classifying ideas
e) brainstorming
f) thinking visually
g) problem solving
h) summarising

i) revising
j) clarifying ideas
k) enhancing memory

THE ORIGIN OF THE MIND MAP

The claim to the origin of the mind map has been made by a popular British psychologist, Tony Buzan. Some of the earliest examples of mind maps were developed by Porphyry of Tyros, a noted thinker of the third century.

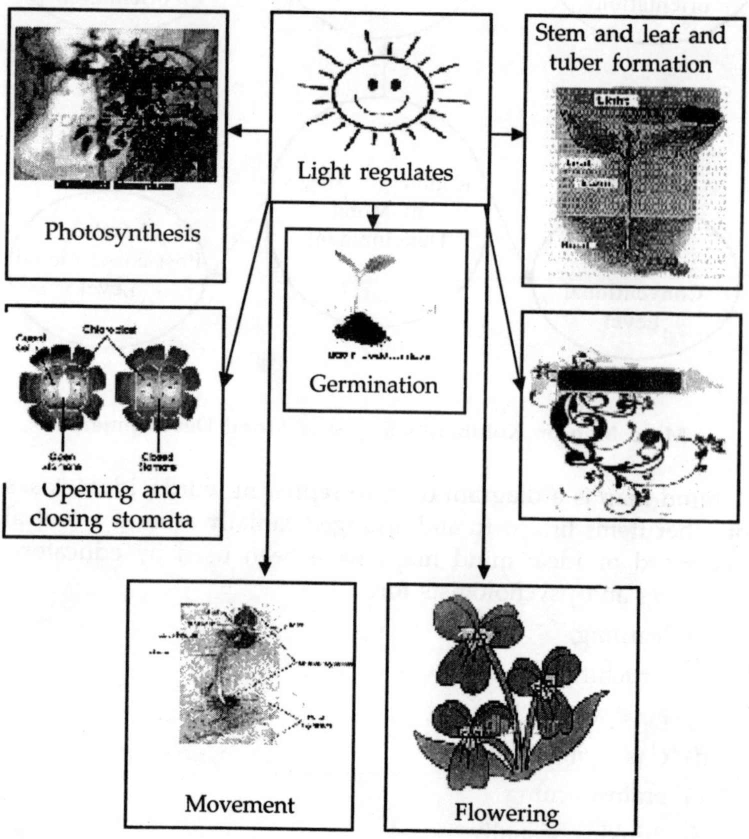

Mind map on the Various Effects of Light on a Green Plant

Kenneth Clark was the first one to talk about Mind Maps in his book 'The Nature of Explanation' (1943). Two other authors who are credited with the use of Mind Maps and whose books (both) titled 'Mental Models' are- Philip Johnson-Laird (1983), a psychology professor at Princeton University and Dedre Gentner and Albert Stevens (1983); though several other authors such as Norman, Krug, Kintsch and Djik elaborated on the use of mental models in their books, it is Buzan who is hailed as the inventor of Mind Maps.

Various Forms and Applications

Mind Maps are an example of 'radiant thinking'. A central idea branches off into many different directions. The branches themselves branch off into finer details or associations. Radiant thinking is both creative and is organised like a tree.

A Mind map is not just a systematic chart of a subject. It is a fun and interesting expression of the way a subject is experienced. It is more important that it is workable and feels right than that it corresponds to any objective standards.

Mind maps provide a way of relating to the world one lives in, a more meaningful way. These are tools for making sense out of anything and for realising one's priorities.

The mind map continues to be used in various forms, and for various applications including learning and education where it is often taught as 'Webs' or 'Webbing' the more popular term being 'thematic webs' in engineering diagramming.

When compared with the earlier original concept map (which was developed by learning experts in the 1960s) the structure of a mind map is a similar, but simplified, radial by having one central key word.

One can also use mind maps as a mnemonic technique or to sort out a complicated idea. Mind maps are also promoted as a way to collaborate in colour pen creativity sessions.

Buzan claims that mind mapping is a superior note-taking method as it has the following advantages:

a) it utilises both right and left hemispheres of the human brain or human cortical skills

b) balances the brain
c) taps into the 99 percent of the unused mental potential
d) taps into the intuition (which he calls "superlogic").

MIND MAP AND ROAD MAP – SIMILARITIES:

a) gives an overview of a large subject/area
b) enables one to plan routes and make choices
c) helps one to know where he /she is going and where one has been
c) enables one to gather and hold large amounts of data
d) encourages problem solving by seeing new creative pathways
e) enables one to be extremely efficient
f) makes it enjoyable to look at, read, muse over and remember
g) attracts and holds the eye/brain

Most often the map involves images, words and lines. The elements are arranged intuitively according to the importance of the concepts and they are organised into groupings, branches, or areas. The uniform graphic formulation of the semantic structure of information on the method of gathering knowledge, may aid recall of existing memory.

Objectives

a) To explore all the creative possibilities of a given subject
b) To clear the mind of previous assumptions about the subject, thus providing space for new creative thought
c) To generate ideas that result in specific action being taken, or physical reality being created or changed
d) To encourage more consistent creative thinking
e) To create new conceptual frameworks within which previous ideas can be reorganised
f) To capture and develop 'flashes' of insight when they occur
g) To plan creatively

Differences of Mind Maps, Concept Maps and Cognitive Maps

Mind Maps	*Concept Maps*	*Cognitive Maps*
This technique is propounded by Busan.	This type of mapping is propounded by Novak).	Cognitive mapping (following Eden and Ackermanns' approach) is based on Personal Construct Theory (Kelly 1955) and it was coined by Tolman.
A mind map has only one main or central concept.	Concept maps may have several focuses.	Cognitive maps are mental representations of spatial information used for navigation.
The mind map structure is "tree like" - branching out from the central idea.	Concept maps are generally complex networks.	In cognitive mapping one is not limited in the number of ideas. While concept mapping "allows" multiple links between ideas, mind mapping typically does not use multiple links between ideas. In cognitive mapping multiple links between ideas are not at all unusual.
A mind map consists of a central word or concept (but preferably a picture), around which ideas that relate to that image are drawn.	Concept maps may have several concepts juxtaposed.	Cognitive maps are used to structure and store spatial knowledge.

(Contd...)

(Contd...)

Mind Maps	*Concept Maps*	*Cognitive Maps*
In a mind map links are usually "passive", not representing anything more than association.	In Concept mapping, two or more concepts are linked by words that describe the hierarchy of concepts.	Cognitive mapping is a technique that was designed primarily for issue/problem structuring, in the context of action-orientated strategic management interventions.
The ideas in mind maps are often single words, which in the case of mind maps, are usually chosen to improve retention in one's memory.	In concept maps the links are labeled with descriptions, defining the association between concepts.	The benefits of the analysis functions are important - without them it is hard to efficiently manage and draw conclusions from large, complex maps.

Advantages of Mind Mapping

Planning

Mind maps help learners in orchestrating all details and aspects of information - from beginning to end - on one piece of paper.

Organising

Mind maps facilitate anyone to have all details at fingertips be it parties, holidays, projects, or any other subject.

Gaining an Overview

It enables the learners to see the whole picture, the global view, at once and understand the links and connections.

Facilitates Learning

Mind maps reduce the burden of huge volumes of work and create the ideal psychological atmosphere and make the readers feel good about study, revision and exams and help learners to have confidence in their learning abilities.

Focusing

Mind maps help learners to concentrate on the relevant and important tasks for better results, using all the cortical skills.

Presenting

While presenting the facts, it enables the learners to express the ideas in a clear, relaxed and lively manner.

Communicating

Mind maps help in communicating ideas with clarity and conciseness, leaving redundant and unnecessary details.

Meetings

From planning the agenda, to chairing, to taking the minutes... the jobs are completed with speed and efficiency.

Facilitation

From preparation to presentation, mind maps make the job easier and much faster.

Manipulation

Mind maps enable learners to have all information on a topic and the learner's current status and how the information can be further manipulated.

Brainstorming

It facilitates brain-storming in which more thoughts are generated and appropriately assessed

Wholeness/Gestalt

Harnessing the brain's tendency to function in gestalt or whole, allows the addition of blank lines to the key words on the Mind Map, enticing the brain to 'fill in' the beckoning areas. Once the brain realises it can associate anything with anything else, it will almost instantaneously find associations, especially when given the trigger of an additional stimulus.

Reviewing

Mind maps enable learners to recall whatever they have learnt and memorise the information in their mind's eye or visually.

The Laws of Mind Mapping

a) selection of the topic, problem or subject matter

b) starting in the centre with an image of the topic, using colors. (Mind maps use pictures or images)

c) Using images, symbols, codes and dimension throughout – using plenty of images helps the learner to associate the idea with the picture or graph (picturisation helps the learner to retain the information and enhances the learner's memory; color, form, line, dimension, texture, visual clues help the learner to think better)

d) Selecting key words and print, using upper or lower case letters - single strong words and meaningful phrases can convey the same meaning more potently

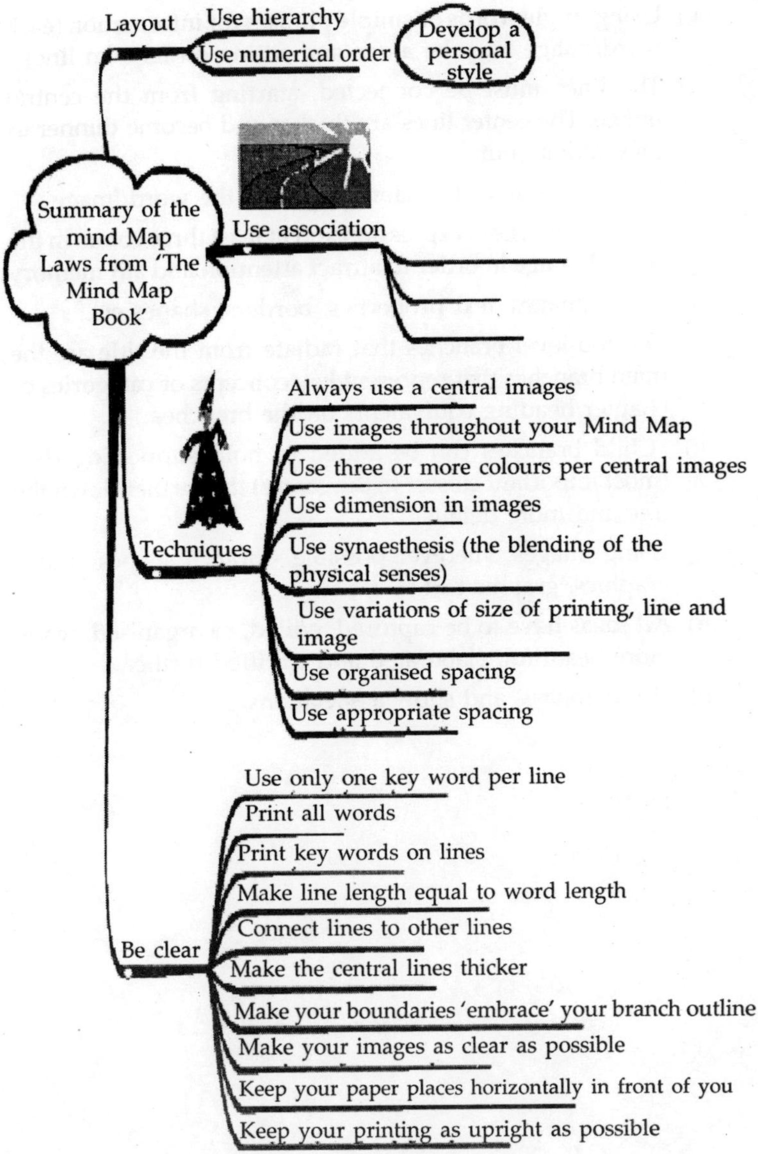

Mind Map of Mind Mapping Laws.

Reference: "The Mind Map Book" by Tony Buzan

e) Using single words or simple phrases for information (each word/image must be alone and sitting on its own line)

f) The lines must be connected, starting from the central image. The center lines are thicker and become thinner as they radiate out.

g) Making the lines the same length as the word/image

h) Using dimension, expression and at least three colors in the central image in order to attract attention and aid memory

i) Using images, text properties, borders, shapes etc.

j) The top-level branches that radiate from the title are the main branches that represent key concepts or categories or chapter heading equivalents on the branches.

k) Child branches can be added to hold supporting data (most important closest to the centre) the further down the tree and more details.

l) Using images wherever possible - branch shapes. attach graphics, graphic text.

m) All ideas have to be captured, edited, re-organised, made more beautiful, elaborated and clarified further.

n) Use emphasis and show associations.

5

Concept Mapping

Chapter Overview

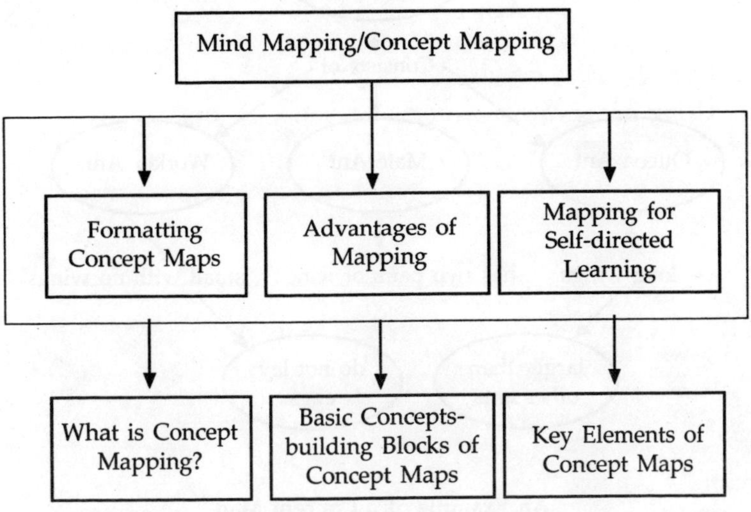

What is Concept Mapping?

Concepts are words or ideas that represent events, objects, or even emotions and feelings. Concept map is a specific kind of mental model for representing and measuring an individual's knowledge. In the learning process, students can develop concept maps as an alternative to traditional note-taking by building associations of non-linear key concepts and organising them to fit with their individual learning styles and frames of reference.

Concept mapping enables people to visualise both the specific relationships among concepts and the hierarchical structure and organisation of these relationships. Concept maps are alternative tools for teaching through building relevant associations among concepts and are visual representations of conceptual relationship. Concept mapping is a process by which an individual acquires, codes, stores, recalls, and decodes information about the relative locations and attributes of a phenomenon in their everyday spatial environment.

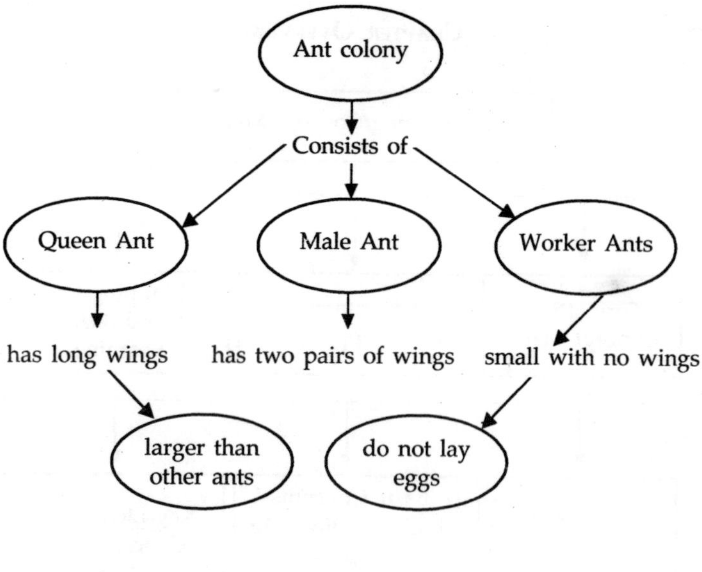

An Example of a Concept Map

Concept maps look like a spider web, consisting of many nodes (i.e., key concepts) connected to one another by lines that indicate relationships. Concepts are located in rectangles or other geometric forms. Concepts can be represented by single key words or phrases or simple drawings. Arcs are lines used to connect the concepts. Concepts are connected with labelled arrows, in a downward-branching hierarchical structure. The relationships among concepts are made explicit and articulated in linking phrases, e.g., 'gives rise to', 'results in', 'is required by', 'contributes to'. Links can be non-directional, unidirectional or bidirectional (the links between the concepts can be one-way, two-way, or non-directional). The concepts and the links may be categorised, and the concept map may show logical relationships among concepts.

Concept mapping serves several purposes. Basically a concept map is the graphical representation of the structure of knowledge. Knowledge graphs are networks of concepts. Networks consist of nodes (points/vertices) and links (arcs/edges). Nodes represent concepts and links represent the relations between concepts. The interconnections between concepts give rise to the power of the concept map. More interconnections and cross-linkages are an indication of a greater complexity and refinement and sophistication of understanding. Concept maps are primarily used in a classroom as teaching aids. It facilitates holistic learning.

Concept map analysis comes in many forms. For course assessments, the analysis may consist of

a) counting the total number of concepts learnt on a particular topic
b) counting the total number of relationships among the concepts
c) measuring the map complexity (number of indicated relationships beyond the minimum
d) needed to connect all concepts linearly – i.e., number of concepts minus one),
e) comparing the maps to that of an expert or an instructor
f) comparing the maps from the beginning or middle of the semester to the maps created at the end of the semester.

These highly quantitative analyses can be combined with more qualitative analyses that seek to understand how concepts are mapped and where they appear on the map.

Steps Involved in Concept Mapping

Six steps are involved:

1) Preparation involves selection of subject matter or the concept to be developed and participants (if it is group work)
2) Generation of ideas and statements

3) Phrasing and structuring of statements
4) Representation of statements in the form of a concept map
5) Interpretation of maps
6) Utilisation of maps.

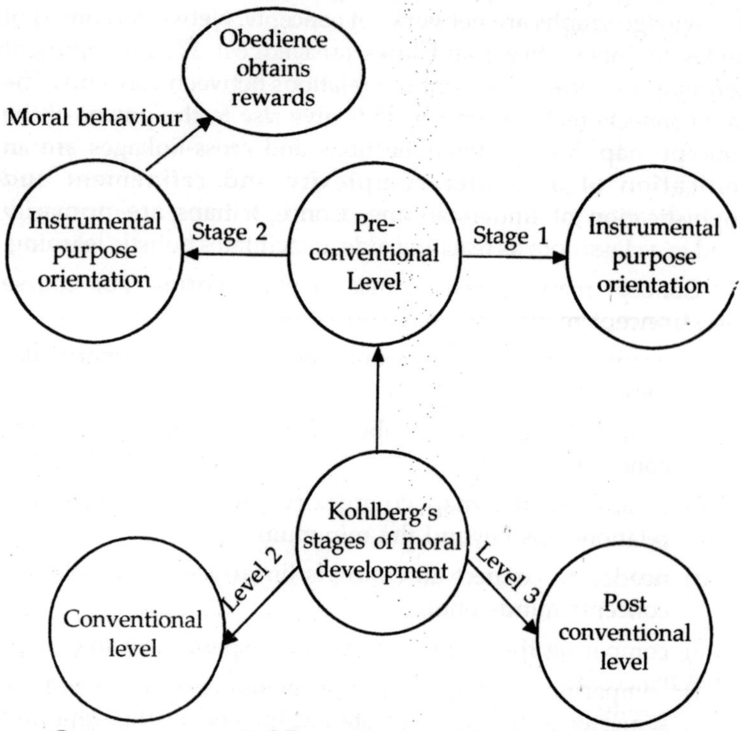

Concept map on Kohlberg's Stages of Moral Development

There are remarkable differences between mind maps and concept maps; mind maps are restricted to radial hierarchies and tree structures. In concept mapping, various forms and multiple hubs and clusters are used. An important point of contrast lies in speed and spontaneity. Mind maps enjoy the advantage of speed and spontaneity. Mind maps depict learner's reflections on a single topic or concept whereas concept maps reflect learner's set of concepts or mental schema.

Purposes of Concept Mapping

Concept mapping can be done for several purposes:

a) to generate ideas (brain storming, etc.);
b) to design a complex structure (long texts, hypermedia, large web sites, etc.);
c) to communicate complex ideas;
d) to aid learning by explicitly integrating new and old knowledge;
e) to assess understanding or diagnose misunderstanding.

Concept maps also known as Idea maps, are verbal-spatial representations of ideas and the relationships connecting them, can resemble flowcharts, diagrams, or tables.

Basic Concepts – Building Blocks of Concept Maps

Concept mapping is a technique for representing knowledge in a graph that is developed to promote and enhance purposeful learning. Concept mapping was originally developed as a research technique. In the 1960s, Joseph D. Novak, at Cornell University, began to study the concept mapping technique. His work was based on the theories of David Ausubel (1968), who stressed the importance of prior knowledge in learning new concepts. Novak concluded that meaningful learning involves the assimilation of new concepts and propositions into existing cognitive structures.

One of the tenets of Ausubel's theory of learning is that the chances of meaningful learning are increased if the learner is presented with an 'advance organiser'.

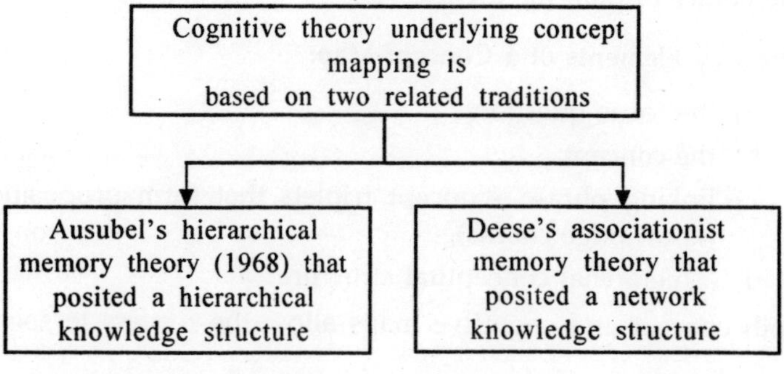

Ausubel's Hierarchical Memory Theory or Hierarchical Concept Map provides a basis whereby Novak and his colleagues worked from and coined the term 'concept map'. Concept maps are intended to 'tap into a learner's cognitive structure and to externalise it'. It is recognised that not all concepts or proposition can be represented. Thus, such maps only provide a 'workable representation'.

Deese's Associationist Memory Theory or Network Concept Maps on the other hand provide a beginning for characterising cognitive structure as a set of concepts and their interrelations. Concepts are represented as nodes in a network linked by the associative overlap of two concepts. This theory acts as the basis for an indirect approach to elicit representations of cognitive structure such as word associations, similarity judgments, and tree building. Such methods produce networks with unlabeled lines. This network characterisation led naturally to the current view of propositional knowledge known as the 'semantic network' with concept nodes linked directionally by labeled arrows to produce propositions.

While both theories started off based on different perspectives, both played a key part that led to the development of concept map from which student's knowledge structures are inferred.

More importantly, we see concept mapping techniques as one effective means to provide the provision of self-directed learning. Besides self-directed learning, evidences point out how concept maps can be used to support learner-centered learning and the enhancement of learning experiences such as self-reflection, stimulation and learner's motivation, learning independence and the ability to plan for themselves.

The Key Elements of a Concept Map:

a) the focus question
b) the concept
c) linking phrase—concept triplets that form propositions (knowledge claims),
d) a hierarchal conceptual structure.

Both concept and cognitive maps allow the readers to see the connections between ideas; to connect new ideas; and to organise ideas in a logical but flexible structure.

Formatting Concept Maps

a) Concept Maps are graphical representations of knowledge comprised of concepts and relationships between them; concept maps graphically illustrate relationships between and among concepts. In a concept map, two or more concepts are linked by words that describe their relationship.

b) Concepts are usually enclosed in circles / boxes (or other geometric forms), and the relationships between the concepts are indicated by connecting lines that link them together.

c) Graphically, it consists of nodes and labeled lines which represent some important aspect of a learner's propositional knowledge in a subject area. The node corresponds to important terms or concepts in the subject area or domain while the lines are connecting links that indicate the relationships between two concepts.

d) A good concept map lends itself to cross-links between concepts

e) In a concept map the nodes are labeled with descriptive text - a word or short phrase representing the concept, and the links are labeled to express a relationship type; crosslinks are an important element because conceptual knowledge is highly relational.

f) Novak and his research team included color, and other formatting features to make concept maps more interesting; use of color and other formatting elements can provide additional cognitive supports to enhance the effectiveness of a concept map, that it can foster meaningful learning. A concept map may be thus customised to enhance communication and understanding.

Guidelines for Doing the Map

a) The main idea in the form of a word or a phrase has to be written in the centre of the page. A circle can be drawn around this to highlight its importance.

b) Related ideas can be placed on branches that radiate from this central idea. Writing in capitals will add clarity and facilitate easy reading and enable the learner to keep the points or phrases brief and to the point.

c) Using unlined or blank paper is recommended; since the presence of lines on paper may hinder the non-linear process of mapping and distract or interfere with the user's thinking process.

d) All words or phrases should be linked with lines to the centre or to other branches. When a new idea is added, a new "spoke" from the centre can be started again. Arrows can be used to join ideas from different branches

e) Colours can be used to group inter-related ideas.

Some Organisational Patterns that may Appear in a Concept Map

Branches —an idea may branch many times to include both closely and distantly related ideas.

Nodes (points/vertices) – Nodes represent concepts.

Arcs/edges – to establish links and these links represent the relations between concepts; links can be non-, uni- or bi-directional.

Arrows—arrows can be drawn to join ideas from different branches.

Groupings—If a number of branches contain related ideas, draw a circle around the whole area.

Lists – (explanatory/exploratory notes) a few sentences as explanatory notes can be added in the map itself, to explain, question, or comment on some aspect of the map — for example, the relationship between some of the ideas.

Advantages of Mapping

a) A concept map is a teaching aid by which connections and relations, as well as the hierarchy of concepts, are presented in an obvious way.

b) It can help students to understand how concepts are linked, how one develops out from another, all of which enable students to extend and deepen their knowledge

c) It clearly defines the central idea, by positioning it in the centre of the page.

d) It allows the user to indicate clearly the relative importance of each idea.

e) It allows the user to figure out the links among the key ideas more easily. This is particularly important for creative work such as essay writing.

f) It allows the learner/user to see all the basic information on one page.

g) As a result of the above, and because each map will look different, it makes recall and review more efficient.

h) It allows the user to add in new information without messy scratching out or squesing in.

i) It makes it easier for the user to see information in different ways, from different viewpoints or angles because it does not lock it into specific positions.

j) It allows the learner to see complex relationships among ideas, such as self-perpetuating systems with feedback loops, rather than forcing the learner to fit non-linear relationships to linear formats.

k) It allows the learner to see contradictions, paradoxes, and gaps in the material — or in his/her own interpretation of it — more easily, and in this way provides a foundation for questioning, which in turn encourages discovery and creativity.

l) Concept maps encourage understanding by helping students organise and enhance their knowledge on any topic. They help students learn new information by integrating each new idea into their existing body of knowledge.

m) Concept maps are ideal for measuring the growth of student learning. As students create concept maps, they reiterate ideas using their own words.

Concept Mapping for Self-Directed Learning

a) Concept mapping techniques are effective means to pave way for self-directed learning.

b) Concept maps can be used to support learner-centered learning and the enhancement of learning experiences.

c) Concept mapping connects the learner with the content or the subject and it makes learning learner-centred.

d) The usage of concept maps promotes self-reflection through its explicit structural model.

e) The important learning factors of motivation and persistence can also be catered for by concept mapping.

f) Concept maps help learners think holistically as they work to understand the inter-relatedness of ideas.

(Adapted from Buzan, T. & Buzan, B. (2000). The Concept Map Book, London, BBC Worldwide Ltd).

6

Cognitive Maps

Chapter Overview

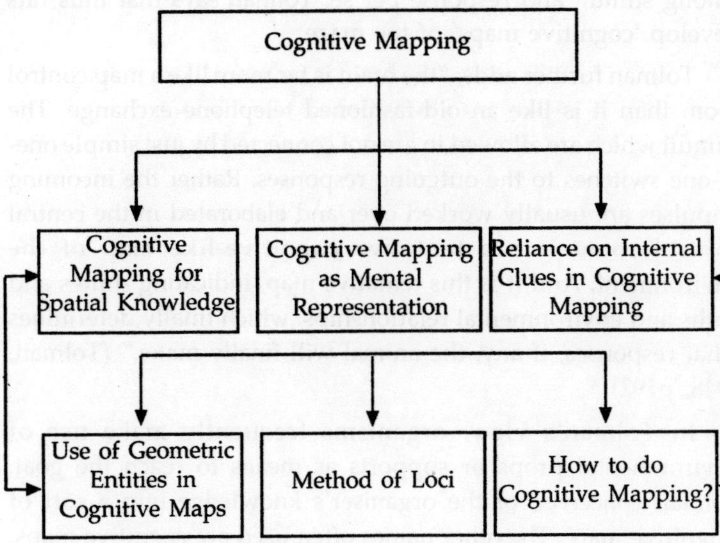

Cognitive Mapping for Spatial Knowledge

Cognitive mapping refers to the means through which individuals process their environment, solve problems using memory; cognitive mapping is a form of memory, but yet, it is much more than that. Cognitive mapping is based on Personal Construct

Theory. 'Cognition' is a psychological construct used to refer to the mental models, or belief systems that people use to perceive, contextualize, simplify, and make sense of otherwise complex problems.

Tolman is credited with the creation of the term "cognitive map"; Tolman developed and expanded 'purposive' theory of learning. His theory deemphasises Pavlovian conditioning as the prime model for the learning process and replaces it with his model of 'sign learning'. Tolman is known for conducting several experiments using rats in mazes. He firmly says that animals usually learn the succession of stimuli or signs that lead to or signify the goal. Tolman's theory suggests the notion that organisms learn relations among stimuli rather than relations among stimuli and response per se. Tolman says that thus rats develop 'cognitive maps' of the maze.

Tolman further adds, "the brain is far more like a map control room than it is like an old-fashioned telephone exchange. The stimuli which are allowed in are not connected by just simple one-to-one switches to the outgoing responses. Rather the incoming impulses are usually worked over and elaborated in the central control room into a tentative cognitive-like map of the environment. And it is this tentative map, indicating routes and paths and environmental relationships, which finally determines what responses, if any, the animal will finally make." (Tolman, 1948, p192)

In Tolman's view, organisms frequently make use of environmental props or supports as means to reach the goal. Tolman conceived of the organiser's knowledge into a sort of 'cognitive map'. The other names often used are cognitive maps, scripts, schemata, and frames of reference.

Cognitive Mapping as Mental Representation

Coined by Tolman, a mental representations of spatial information used for navigation are called cognitive maps.

Downs and Stea in their textbook 'Cognitive Mapping and Spatial Behavior' (1973) define cognitive mapping as "A process composed of a series of psychological transformations by which an individual acquires, codes, stores, recalls, and decodes information about the relative locations and attributes of phenomena in their everyday spatial environment."

The purpose of the cognitive map is to integrate and apply environmental information using a representation that is built inside the head for the individual's personal use.

Reliance on Internal Clues in Cognitive Mapping

As an individual's familiarity with an area increases, he/she makes use of the internal cognitive map and he/she gradually reduces the reliance on external sources of information. For example, after having walked from the school to the train station numerous times, the tracks become less of a common representation of the vicinity of the train station, but more of an anticipated landmark used in the process of localisation within the cognitive map. In Tolman's view, behaviour frequently makes use of environmental props or supports as means-objects toward the goal. Tolman conceived of the organism's knowledge as organised into a sort of 'cognitive map' of the environment rather than being a simple listing of local stimulus-response pairs.

Cognitive maps store conscious perceptions, but also automatic (subconscious) encodings of spatial relations to help determine one's current position, where specific objects are in surrounding space, and how to get from one place to another. This type of internal representation is also known as a subjective structure, a mental map, a cognitive collage, a cognitive configuration.

Use of Geometric Entities in Cognitive Maps

Cognitive maps are representations of sets of connected places, which are systematically related by groups of spatial transformation rules. Despite the name, cognitive maps are not similar to cartographic maps.

Cognitive representations need not bear a one-to-one correspondence with their counterparts in physical space, and evidence shows that cognitive maps can violate basic geometric axioms (Rivizzigno 1976).

Furthermore, Golledge suggests that if cognitive maps were cartographically founded, map reading skills would be required prior to the use of cognitive maps. However, studies have shown the skill of map reading to be acquired in children development well after the child exhibited use of a cognitive map.

Cognitive Maps: Method of Loci

The oldest known formal method of using spatial locations to remember data is the method of loci. This method was originally used by students of rhetoric in ancient Rome while memorising speeches.

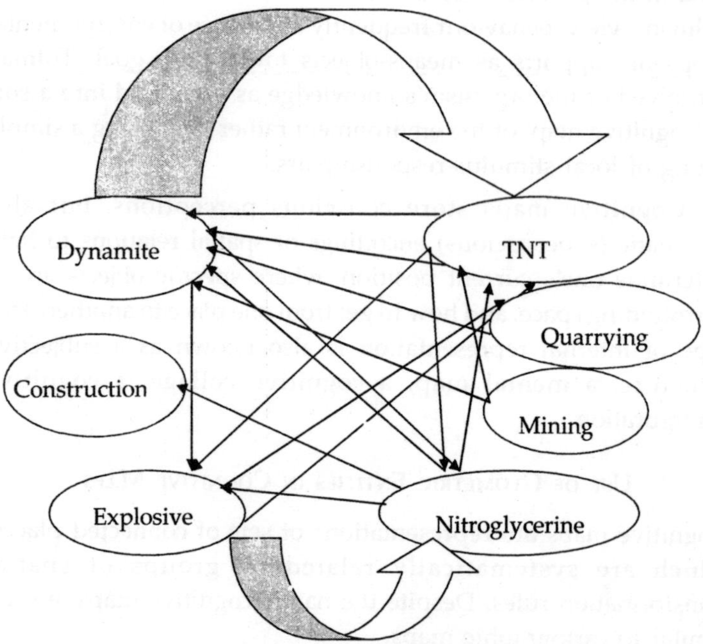

Cognitive Map of Dynamite and its Applications

To use it one must first memorise the appearance of a physical location (for example, the sequence of rooms in a building). When a list of words, for example, needs to be memorised, the learner visualises an object representing that word in one of the pre-memorised locations. To recall the list, the learner mentally "walks through" the memorised locations, noticing the objects placed there during the memorisation phase.

Cognitive maps may also be represented and assessed on paper or screen through various practical methods such as a concept map, sketch map, spider diagram or any variety of spatial representation.

How to do Cognitive Mapping

In cognitive mapping, as with the other forms of mapping, the full meaning of the ideas is given by the "whole picture". Links between ideas add further contextual information to the concepts themselves, and there is meaning through the content of the ideas - the way in which they are expressed as short phrases - and through the context within which they sit.

While concept mapping "allows" multiple links between ideas, mind mapping typically does not use multiple links between ideas. In cognitive mapping multiple links between ideas are not at all unusual and there is no limitation on the number of links between concepts.

Cluster Analysis is used to identify groups of concepts that are tightly linked together, which typically cover a particular area of the issue being mapped.

Spoke structures are indicative of "learning-readiness"; chain structures are indicators of "goal-orientation" and networks are indicators of expertise. Furthermore, change that comprises simple elaboration of existing spokes or chains is likely to be the result of surface learning styles and the emergence of networks indicative of deep learning.

Conclusion

The cognitive mapping technique is not directly comparable to mind mapping or concept mapping. The technique was designed primarily for issue/ problem structuring, in the context of action orientated strategic management interventions. The technique can be used with individuals and when working with groups. Although it was designed, initially, to support a particular form of mapping (cognitive mapping), there are many different ways in which it can be used.

7

Organisational Patterns of Concepts

Chapter Overview

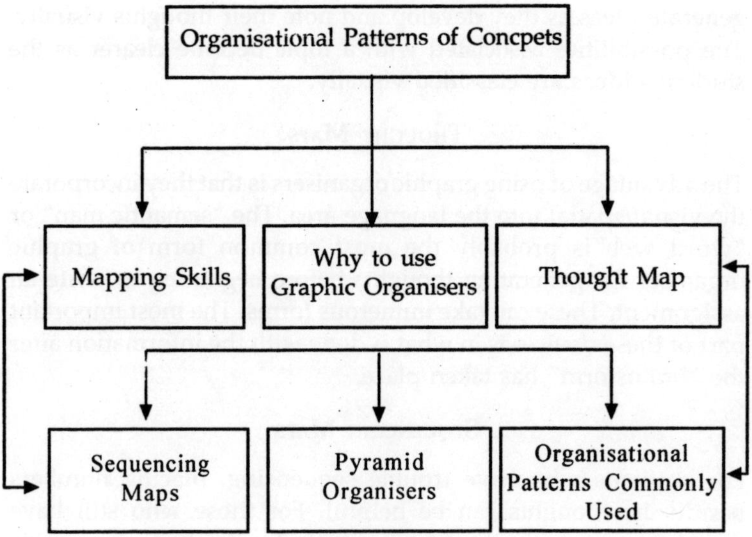

Mapping Skills

There are many similar names for graphic organisers including: knowledge maps, concept maps, story maps, entity relationship charts, mind maps, cognitive organisers, advance organisers etc., it is a pictorial way of constructing knowledge and organising information. Mapping skills help students to convert and compress a lot of seemingly disjointed information into a structured, simple-to-read, graphic display. The resulting visual display conveys complex information in a simple-to-understand manner.

Increasing Understanding by Creating Graphic Organisers

The process of converting a mass of data/information/ideas into a graphic map gives the student an increased understanding and insight into the topic at hand. To create the map, the student must concentrate on the relationships between the items and examine the meanings attached to each of them. While creating a map, the student must also prioritise the information, determining which parts of the material are the most important and should be focused upon, and where each item should be placed in the map.

The creation of graphic organisers also helps the student generate ideas as they develop and note their thoughts visually. The possibilities associated with a topic become clearer as the student's ideas are classified visually.

Thought Maps

The advantage of using graphic organisers is that they incorporate the visual/spatial into the language area. The "semantic map" or "word web"is probably the most common form of graphic organiser for generating thoughts before beginning to write an assignment. These can take numerous forms. The most important part of these devices is in what is done with the information after the "brainstorm" has taken place.

Sequencing Maps

For students who have trouble sequencing, placing numbers beside the thoughts can be helpful. For those who still have trouble arranging the thoughts in a logical way, place a few words to represent each thought on a separate piece of paper. Arrange them into possibilities and orally state the material in sequence. When it makes the most sense, number each thought, and then proceed to the rough draft of writing.

Pyramid Organisers

After the main brainstorming has been done, another way to organise thoughts is to connect main ideas to supporting details. The top of the pyramid is the topic. Next is an explanation of the main idea. Under that is supporting ideas or further explanation in details - three or four, followed underneath by examples. Many formats for graphic organisers have been published so far covering different areas of knowledge.

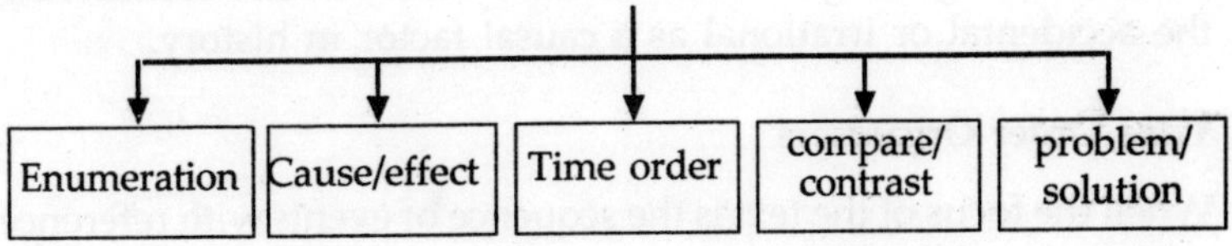

Organisational Patterns Commonly Used

Recognition of text pattern has been found to be a key strategy for comprehension and retention (Smith, 1964). However, this can be a difficult skill for students because authors do not always write in a clearly identifiable pattern. Often several patterns can be found within a single text. Teachers are encouraged to model how to analyse the overall organisation of a selection by looking for explicit signal words that indicate a pattern that ties the ideas together (Vacca & Vacca, 1986). Graphic organisers can then be used to illustrate the major relationships in the top-level structure and to sort out the important from the less important ideas.

A powerful way to do a chapter summary for a novel study or a summary of a short story is to place the title in the centre of a blank page, then going in a circle around the centre, sequence the main events through sketches of who, what, why, where, when.

Problem/Solution Organisers

The problem/solution text structure is a common pattern that is easily identified. Students summarise the text as they fill in the graphic organiser. Texts with more than one problem can branch into additional frames.

Compare/Contrast Organisers

Students are often asked to find likenesses (compare) and differences (contrast) among facts, people, events, or concepts. The compare / contrast graphic organiser can help students to organise their points.

Cause / effect Structure

Cause/effect text shows how events, facts, or concepts happened to come into being because of other facts, events, or concepts. The leamer will work forward from some initiating event to its outcome recognising cause and effect factors but also considering the accidental or irrational as a causal factor in history.

Time Order Organisers

When the focus of the text is the sequence of events with reference to time, graphic organisers can aid students in ordering events. One type of time order organiser that many social studies teachers use effectively is a timeline.

Enumeration Organisers

Enumeration structure, the listing of information about a topic, event, object, or person, is probably the most commonly encountered textbook pattern. Vocabulary mapping is an effective method of organising information so that students see relationships among these facts. A semantic web is another type of organiser that allows students to deal with enumeration structure. Students list and categorise information on given topics.

Conclusion

Graphic organisers are simple and effective; they can be completed as a whole group, in small groups, or by individuals. The key to success, however, is the discussion that takes place when students share their reasons for the information they put in the organisers. Stahl and Vancil (1986) compared groups of students who did not discuss their organisers with groups who had discussed and found that the non-discussion students did not show improvement in comprehension, vocabulary, or memory. They concluded that discussion is a critical element in the use of graphic organisers. The overall goal of using graphic organisers in the classroom is that students will begin organising information into their own mental frameworks.

8

Graphic Organisers in the Classroom

Chapter Overview

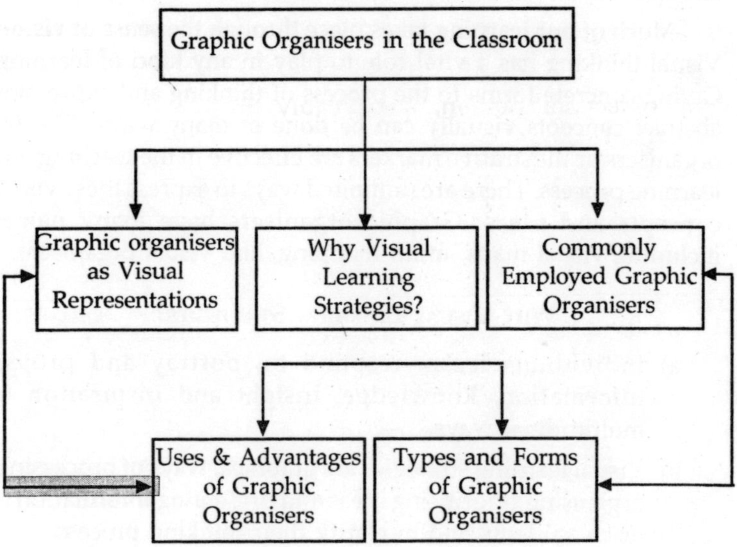

Graphic Organisers as Visual Representations of Concepts

A graphic organiser is a visual representation of concepts, knowledge, or information that can incorporate both text and pictures. Graphic organisers allow the mind 'to see' the undiscovered patterns and relationships. These display information, structure, and key conceptual relationships using visual and spatial arrangements or maps.

Graphic organisers often involve lines, arrows, text boxes or bubbles, pictures, and other visual depictions to represent ideas, facts, and concepts. Graphic organisers provide a framework for students to connect existing knowledge to new information. Some of the most commonly known graphic organisers include semantic maps, semantic feature analysis, cognitive maps, story maps, framed outlines, flow charts, thematic webs, spider maps, bubbles, clusters and Venn diagrams. Graphic organisers have been used in many academic subject areas. Individuals tend to have strengths and inclinations for learning through different modalities or channels. There are 'auditory learners', 'visual learners', 'tactile-kinesthetic learners' and 'analytic and global learners' to name a few.

Much of our learning takes place through the sense of vision. Visual thinking has a vital role to play in any kind of learning. Giving concrete forms to the process of thinking and expressing abstract concepts visually can be done in many ways. Graphic organisers or illustrative markers are effective in the teaching and learning process. There are unlimited ways to express these visual concepts and ideas. Graphic organisers have many names including visual maps, mind mapping, and visual organisers.

Why Visual Learning Strategies?

a) Individuals learn, respond to, portray and project information, knowledge, insight and inspiration in multitudinal ways.

b) Visual learning strategies are graphical ways of processing, organising prioritising ideas and presenting information to teach students and to clarify their thinking process.

c) Visual diagrams reveal patterns, interrelationships and interdependencies.

d) They also stimulate creative thinking.

Graphic organisers in classrooms as visual and organisational tools facilitate student comprehension. Teachers find that graphic organisers improve their presentation of materials; teachers feel that use of graphic organisers increases student comprehension of text; and also that students are more engaged in learning when they participate in the completion of graphic organisers.

Commonly Employed Graphic Organisers

Graphic organisers most commonly employed –

a) structured overviews
b) graphs
c) bars
d) tables
e) columns
f) algorithms
g) diagrams – sequential, conceptual, hierarchical, cyclical, Venn, fishbone or Ishikawa, squeeze and stretch,
h) Charts - why-why, who-what- why-when and how charts, KWL chart, web, mind map, networks and flowcharts

Graphic organisers can be used as a means to assist students in the complex act of making sense of content-area text. Graphic organisers can be effectively used to –

a) analyse
b) sequence
c) classify
d) distinguish
e) compare and contrast
f) make connections
g) develop solutions
h) evaluate
i) interact
j) infer
k) brainstorm
l) summarise

These tactics help learners to:

a) tell a story
b) convey information
c) describe and delineate
d) persuade and influence

e) analyse and understand

f) critically evaluate

Research in both educational theory and cognitive psychology tells us that visual learning is the best method for teaching students of all ages how to think and how to learn.

The use of graphic organisers or mental maps presented in visual form that represent key skills such as sequencing, comparing, contrasting and classifying help learners immensely.

Graphic organisers can be used in all phases of learning from brainstorming ideas to presenting findings.

Graphic organisers have been applied across a range of curriculum subject areas. Although reading is by far the most well studied application, science, social studies, language arts, and math are additional content areas that are represented in the research base on graphic organisers.

Operations such as mapping cause and effect, note taking, comparing and contrasting concepts, organising problems and solutions, and relating information to main ideas or themes can be beneficial to many subject areas.

Uses of Graphic Organisers

Visual learning techniques help students in problem solving, decision making, studying, planning research and brainstorming.

To Clarify Thinking

Learners come to know how ideas are connected, grouped and organised. With visual learning, new concepts are more thoroughly assimilated and easily understood.

To Think Critically and Creatively

Graphic organisers show ways to improve students' abilities to solve problems significantly and to think critically and creatively. These tools help students develop both their analytical capabilities and their academic language skills.

To Reinforce Understanding

Students recreate and review, in their own words, what they've already learned. This helps them absorb, assimilate and internalise new information, giving them ownership of their ideas.

To Integrate and Internalise New Knowledge

Diagrams updated throughout a lesson prompt students to build upon prior knowledge and internalise new information. By reviewing diagrams created previously, students see how to integrate and synthesise knowledge.

ADVANTAGES OF GRAPHIC ORGANISERS

Graphic Organisers

a) facilitate learners in thinking through complex problems
b) help in quick and rapid review
c) relieve learner boredom
d) increase meaningful learning
e) enhance recall
f) provide motivation
g) create interest
h) clarify and overview information
i) assist in organising thoughts
j) promote understanding
k) serve as effective mnemonics
l) relate pieces of information
m) show interrelationships among ideas
n) serve as study guides
o) summaries of text chapters/units
p) locate key facts and ideas
q) remind of key facts and ideas
r) introduce text information
s) rearrange text information

Point of Implementation

Before a new learning situation to set the stage, address prior knowledge, develop background or essential learning and guide thinking.

During a new learning situation to categorise and/or organise information, raise questions for consideration, predict solutions or conclusions;

After a new learning situation, to confirm or reject prior knowledge, relate new information to what is already known, extend new learning to other situations ;

With material already learned, a simple way to organise or outline learning or ideas;

When developing a piece of writing, as an effective means to organise thoughts or ideas.

The process of reviewing information and organising it appears to help learners arrange the material in their minds.

Types of Graphic Organisers

Graphic organisers may be grouped or classified as representing

a) Sequential information,

b) Single main concept

c) Multiple concepts.

Different types within each classification can be used to represent simple or more complex information.

This can be further classified as:

a) Hierarchical organisers, present main ideas and supporting details in ranking order or hierarchy.

b) Comparative organisers, depict similarities and differences among key concepts.

c) Sequential organisers illustrate a series of steps or place events in a chronological order.

d) Diagrams depict actual objects and systems in the real world of science and social studies.

e) Cyclical organisers depict a series of events that have no beginning or end.

f) Conceptual organisers include a main concept with supporting facts, evidence, or characteristics.

Graphic organisers come in many different forms, each one best suited to organising a particular type of information. The following examples are merely a sampling of the different types and uses of graphic organisers.

Forms of Graphic Organisers and their Functions

Applications Across Curriculum Areas

Children organise and make sense of the world around them

Graphic Organiser-Pictorial Representation	*Functions – Description and characterstics of the Graphic Organiser*
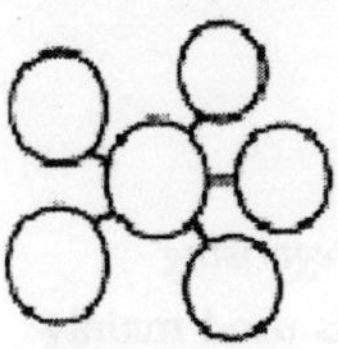 *Bubble Map*	*Describing* Describing different characterstics, qualities, salient features of an organism, an event, a phenomenon.
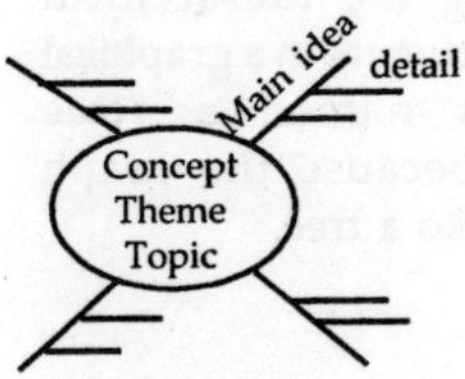 *Spider Map*	*Describing* Spider concept map is organized by placing the central theme or idea in the center with outwardly radiating sub-themes around it.
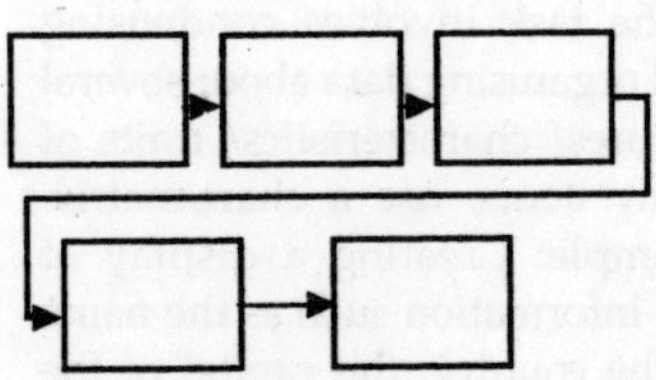 *Flowchart*	*Sequencing* A flowchart illustrates the steps in a process. By visualising the process, a flowchart can quickly help identify bottlenecks or inefficiencies where the process can be streamlined or improved.

(Contd...)

(Contd...)

Graphic Organiser-Pictorial Representation	*Functions – Description and characterstics of the Graphic Organiser*
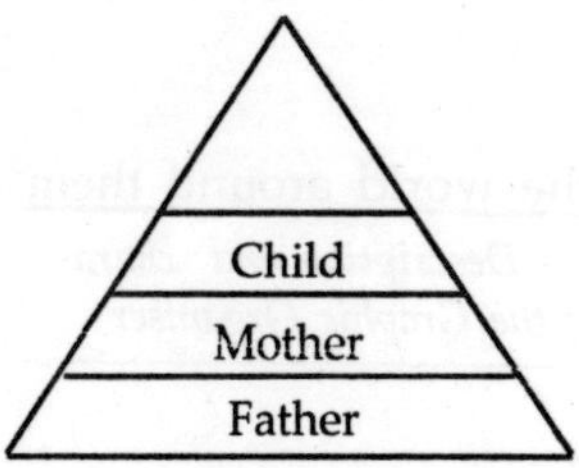 *Hierarchy Map*	*Classifying and Categorising* Hierarchy concept map presents information in a descending order of importance. The most important information is placed at the top.
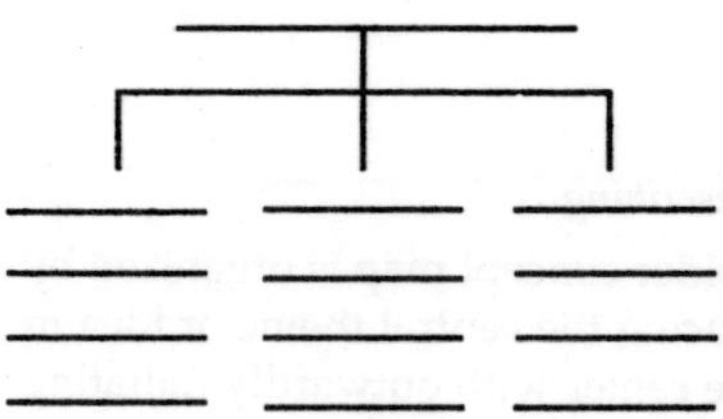 *Tree Map*	*Classsifying and Categorising* This type of chart is used mainly for categorising and classifying. A tree structure is a way of representing the hierarchical nature of a structure in a graphical form. It is named a "tree structure" because the graph looks a bit like a tree.
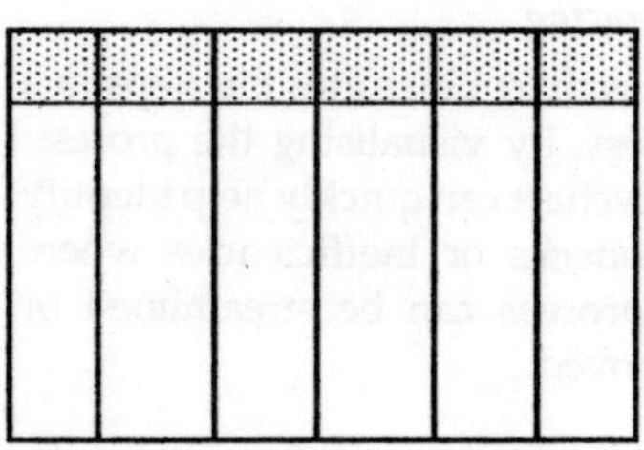 *Chart / Matrix Diagram*	*Classifying and categorising* If the task involves condensing and organising data about several features/ characteristics/ traits of many items, use a chart/matrix. Example: Creating a display of key information such as the name of the country, the capital of the country, important monuments, the chief agricultural produces and industries etc.

(Contd...)

Graphic Organiser-Pictorial Representation	*Functions – Description and characterstics of the Graphic Organiser*
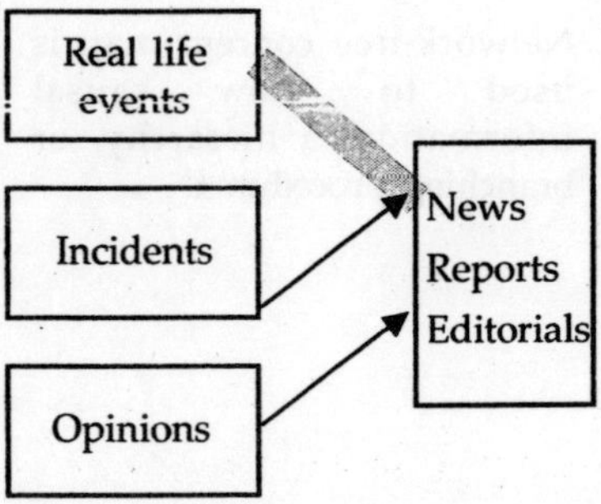 *Systems Concept Map*	*Organising* Systems concept map organises information in a format, which is similar to a flowchart with the addition of inputs and outputs.
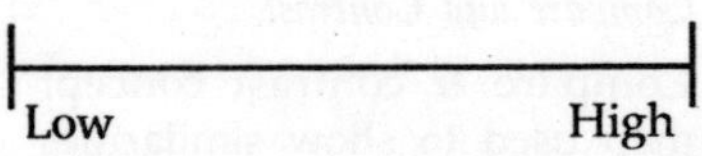 *Continuum Scale*	*Sequencing* Continuum Scale is effective for organising information along a dimension such as less to more, low to high, and few to many. If the topic has definite beginning and ending points, and a number of divisions or sequences in between, use a continuum.
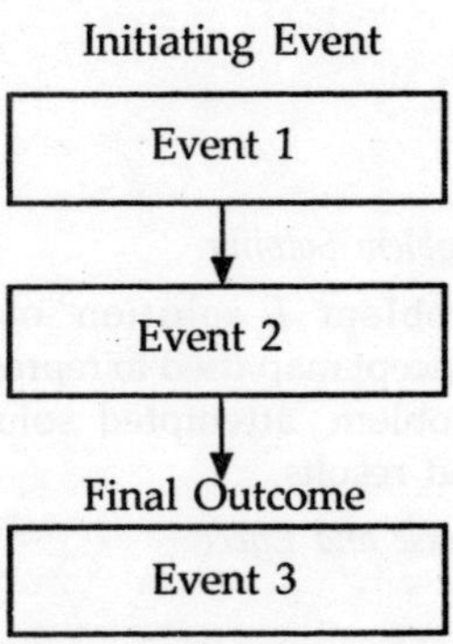 *Series of events chain concept map*	*Sequencing* Series of events chain concept map is used to organise and describe information according to various steps or stages, a sequence of events/the goals, actions and outcomes of a historical figure or character in a novel or the beginning, middle and end of a story.

(Contd...)

(Contd...)

Graphic Organiser-Pictorial Representation	*Functions – Description and characterstics of the Graphic Organiser*
Network Tree 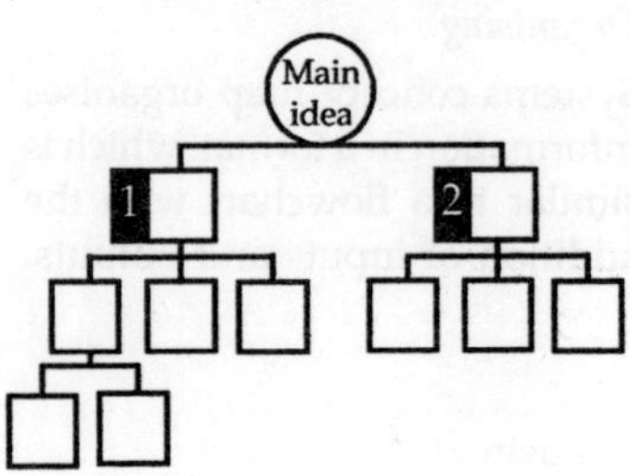 *Network-tree concept map*	*Networking* Network-tree concept map is used to show causal information, a hierarchy, or branching procedures.
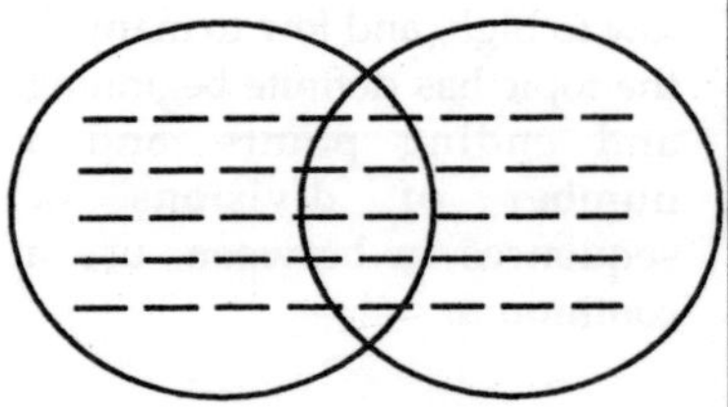 *Venn Diagram*	*Compare and Contrast* Compare & contrast concept map used to show similarities and differences between two things (people, places, events, ideas, etc).
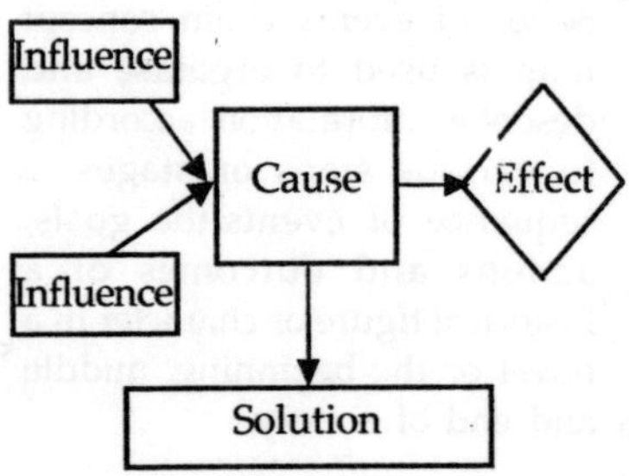 *Problem/solution outline concept map*	*Problem Solving* Problem / solution outline concept map used to represent a problem, attempted solutions and results. *Cause and Effect*

(Contd...)

(Contd...)

Graphic Organiser-Pictorial Representation	*Functions – Description and characterstics of the Graphic Organiser*
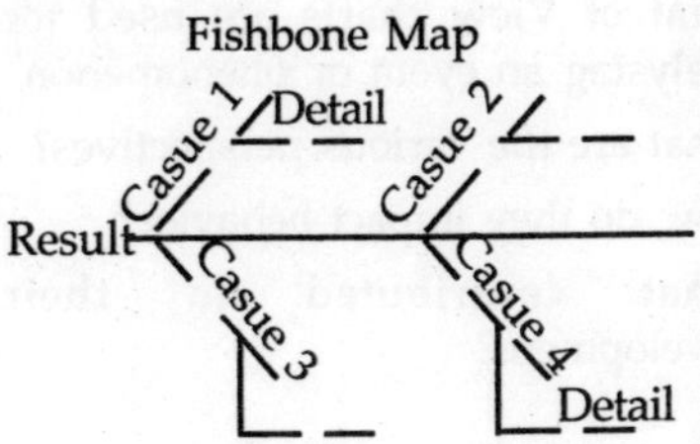 *Ishikawa / Fishbone –map*	*Cause and Effect* When cause-effect relationships are complex and non-redundant a Fishbone-map may be particularly useful. If the topic involves investigating multiple cause-and-effect factors associated with a complex topic and how they inter-relate, using a fishbone diagram will be useful.
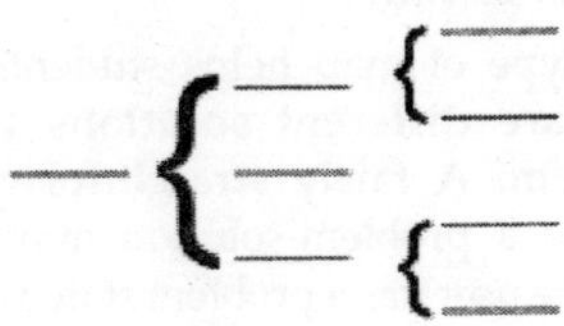 *Bracket Map*	*Bracket Map* Bracket map is used to portray structure – from part to whole What is the whole object or concept? What are the major parts of it? What are the subparts of each major part (if any)?
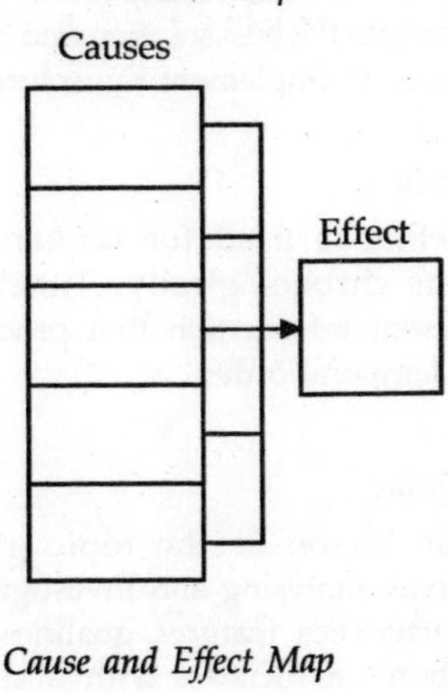 *Cause and Effect Map*	*Cause and Effect - Intervene Map* This map is used to indicate causes and effects of an event or phenomenon What are the causes and effects of this event? What might happen next? This type of map invites readers to make inferences about how one event relates to another, how one event inspires or leads to another. This insight about cause-effect dramatically improves students' reading and thinking, and writing abilities.

(Contd...)

(Contd...)

Graphic Organiser-Pictorial Representation	*Functions – Description and characterstics of the Graphic Organiser*
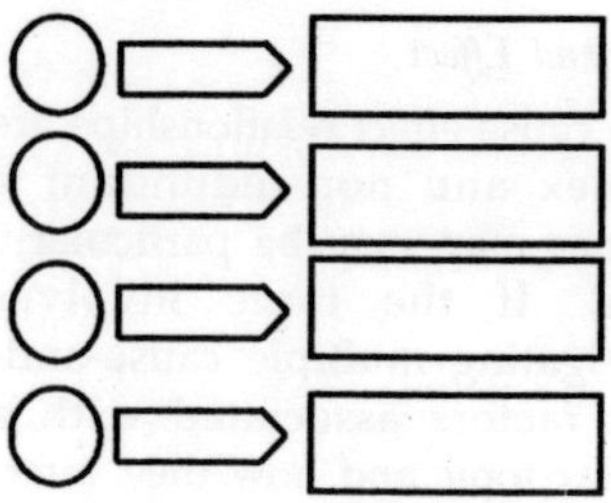 *Point of View*	*Point of View Charts* Point of View charts are used for analysing an event or phenomenon. What are the various perspectives? How do they impact behavior? What contributed to their development?
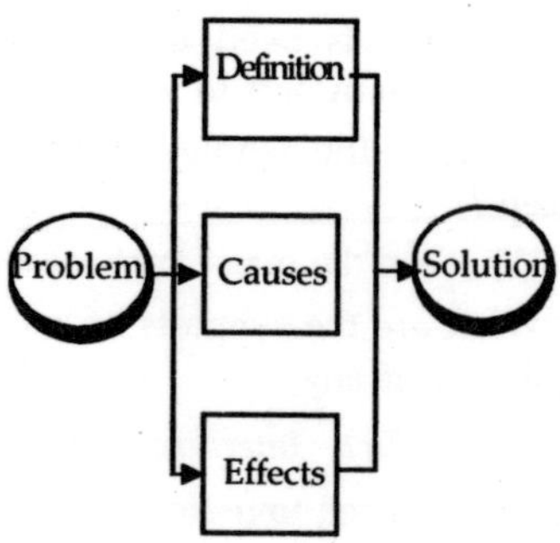 *Problem Solution*	*Problem Solving* This type of map helps students to compare different solutions to a problem. A fairly straightforward map is a problem-solution map. In this, the user has a problem statement, definition, causes, and effects, leading to a possible solution and it also helps to evaluate the best solution and helps the user to implement the solution.
 *Timeline*	*Timeline* Timeline is used for sequencing events chronologically. Timelines represent information that proceeds in a temporal order.
 *Star*	*Analysing* If the lesson or the topic given involves analysing and investigating characteristics, features, qualities and attributes associated with a single

(Contd...)

(Contd...)

Graphic Organiser-Pictorial Representation	*Functions – Description and characterstics of the Graphic Organiser*
	topic, use a star diagram as your graphic organiser. Example: Explaining the physical characteristics of an animai, its habitat, its place in ecology, its classification or zoological name, its uses etc.,
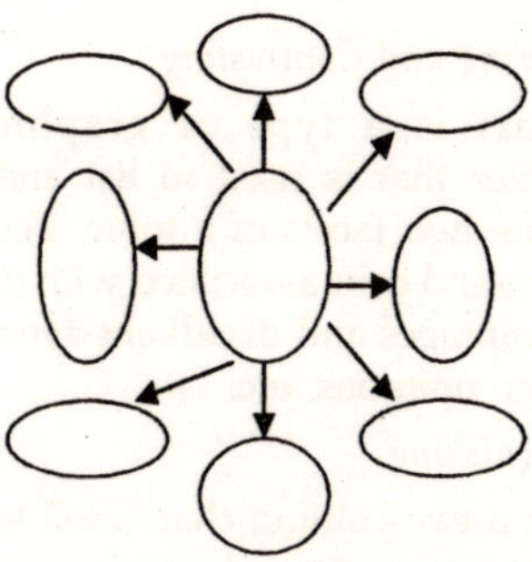 *Cluster /Cloud*	*Generating Ideas* This type of diagram is used to generate and organise ideas in early stages of reading or writing or thinking process. Example: brainstorming.
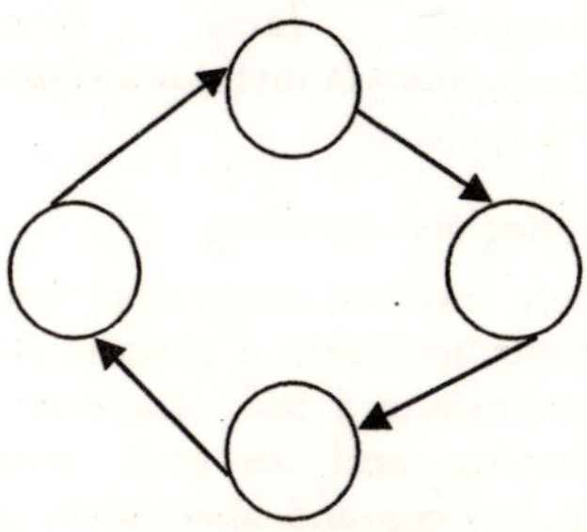 *Cycle Map*	*Describing cycle of events* A Cycle Map is useful for organising information that is circular or cyclical, with no absolute beginning or ending. Example topic: Documenting the stages in the lifecycle of an animal.
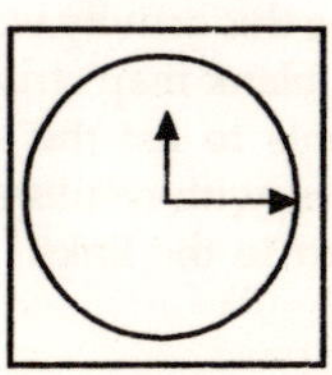 *Clock*	*Sequencing and summarising* This type of diagram is used to describe clock-like cycle. Example topic: Recording the events in a typical school day or making a story clock to summarise a story.

(Contd...)

(Contd...)

Graphic Organiser-Pictorial Representation	*Functions – Description and characterstics of the Graphic Organiser*

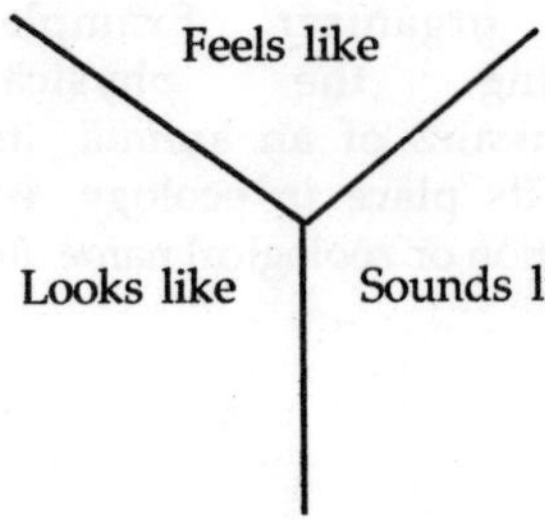

Y-Chart Diagram

Describing

This type of chart is chiefly used to analyse and organise three qualities

Example: describing a character in a book- including what the character looks like, sounds like, and how the character feels.

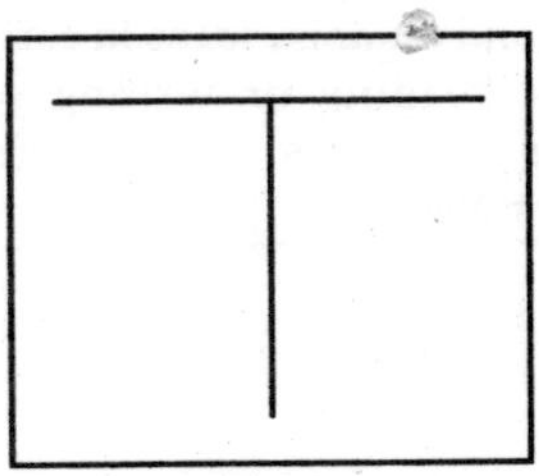

T Charts

Comparing and Contrasting

T Chart is a type of graphic organizer that is used to list and examine two facets of a topic, like the pros and cons associated with it, its advantages and disadvant-ages, facts vs. opinions, etc.

Distinguishing

This is a two-column chart used to evaluate the facts and opinions of an event or a phenomenon or to distinguish facts from misconceptions or myths associated with a topic.

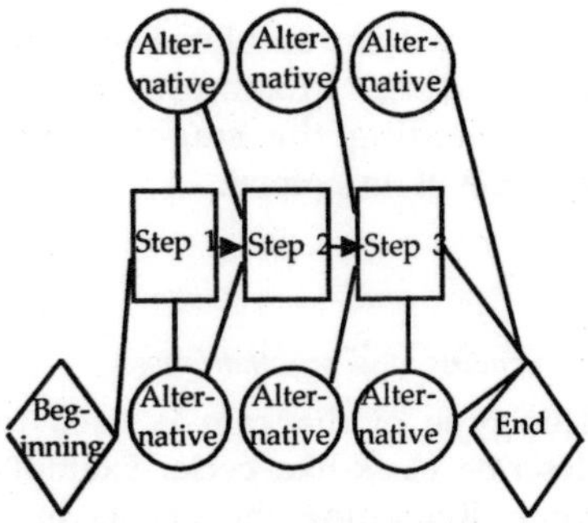

Process Development Map

Analysing and describing

A more involved assignment asks students to create a process for accomplishing a task. There is a beginning and an end, with multiple steps and alternatives at each step. One possible way of structuring this activity would be to provide a blank map structure and ask students to list the steps and alternatives, with results shown by adding text to the links.

(Contd...)

(Contd...)

<table>
<tr><th>Graphic Organiser-Pictorial Representation</th><th>Functions – Description and characterstics of the Graphic Organiser</th></tr>
<tr><td><table><tr><td>Pluses</td><td>Minuses</td><td>Implications</td></tr><tr><td></td><td></td><td></td></tr></table>PMI Chart</td><td>Decision Making
PMI Chart is a type of a three-column graphic organiser in which the learner or decision maker examines the Plusses, Minuses, and Implications or Interesting points associated with a topic, decision, or idea. PMI charts help an individual to evaluate the positive negative and interesting points involved in any concept or problem or decision.</td></tr>
<tr><td><table><tr><td>Know</td><td>Want</td><td>How</td><td>Learn</td></tr><tr><td></td><td></td><td></td><td></td></tr></table>KWHL Diagram</td><td>Analysing and Organising
This 4 column diagram is mainly used to analyse and organise what prior information the learner has about a topic and what more he /she wants to know about the topic.
K stands for what you already KNOW about the subject. W stands for what you WANT to learn. H stands for figuring out HOW you can learn more about the topic. L stands for what you LEARN as you read.</td></tr>
<tr><td>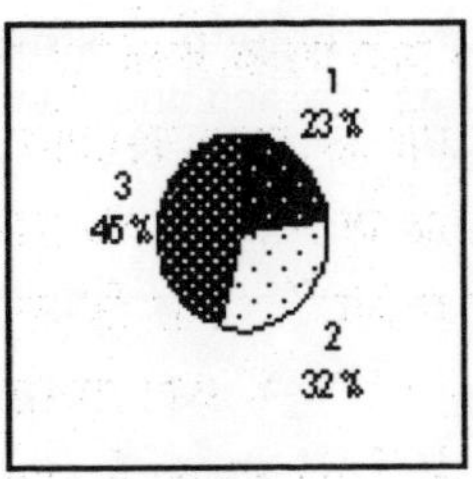Pie Charts</td><td>Delineating
This type of chart is mainly used to portray the divisions within a group or a population. For example drawing a pie chart will be useful to portray how much percentage of a group represents different sections or divisions.</td></tr>
</table>

(Contd...)

(Contd...)

Graphic Organiser-Pictorial Representation	*Functions – Description and characterstics of the Graphic Organiser*

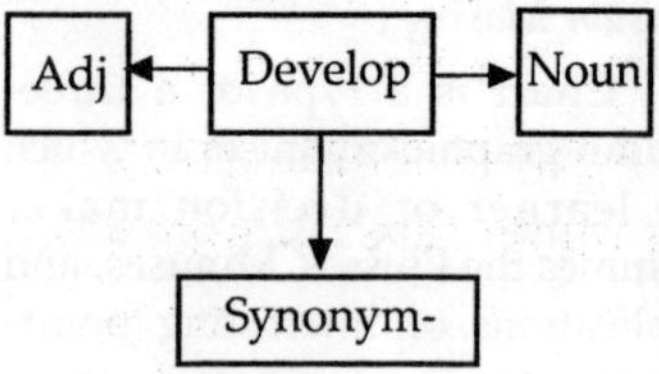

Vocabulary Map

Vocabulary building

Graphic organisers can be useful in helping a student learn new vocabulary words, having them list the word, its part of speech (noun, verb, adjective, adverb, etc.), a synonym, an antonym, a drawing that represents the word, and a sentence using the word.

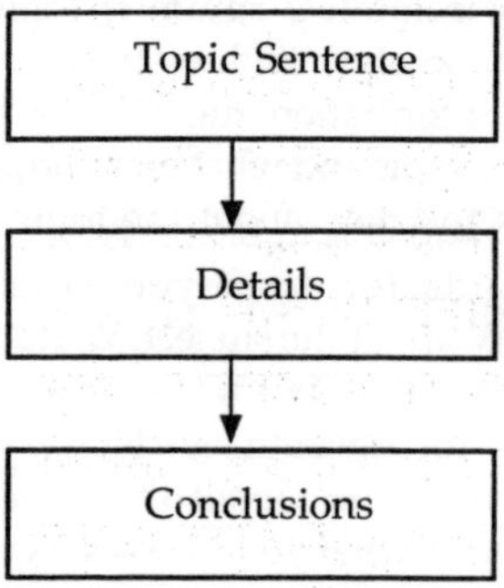

Paragraph Structure

Organising

These graphic organisers help you organise the structure of a paragraph, including a topic sentence, sentences with support details and a conclusion sentence.

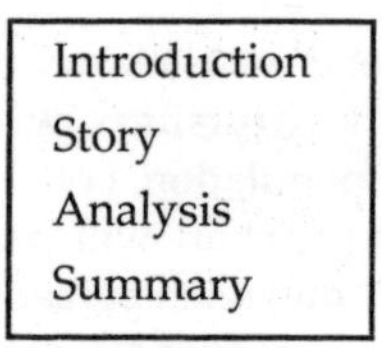

Story Map

Analysing and Understanding

Story maps can help a student summarise, analyse and understand a story or event.

(Contd...)

(Contd...)

Graphic Organiser-Pictorial Representation	*Functions – Description and characterstics of the Graphic Organiser*
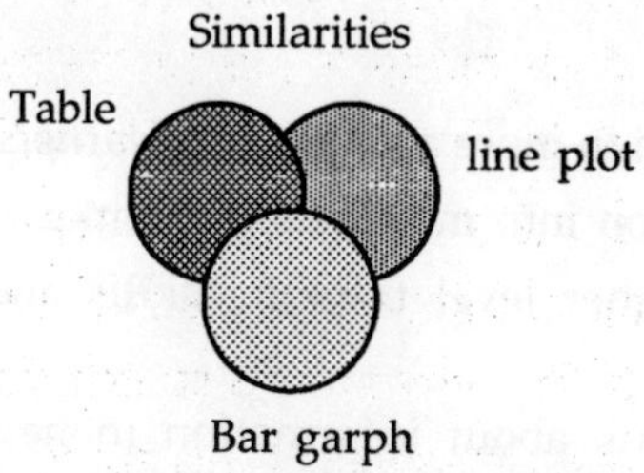 *Compare and Contrast Map*	*Compare and Contrast Map* Compare and contrast concept maps are used to show similarities and differences between two or more things (people, places, events, ideas, etc).
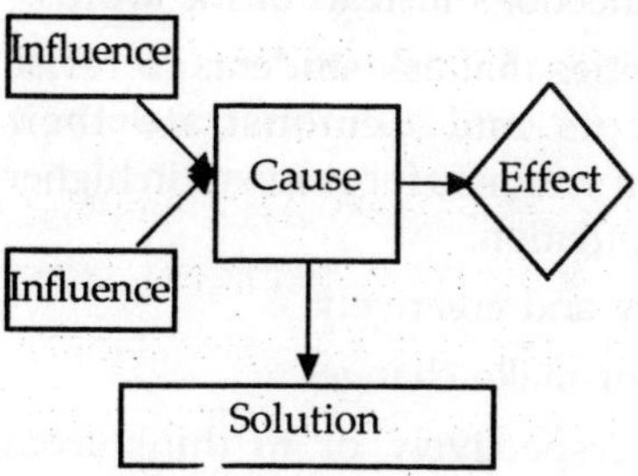 *Problem/solution outline concept map*	*Problem / Solution Map* Problem / solution outline concept map is used to represent a problem, attempted solutions and results (the national debt).
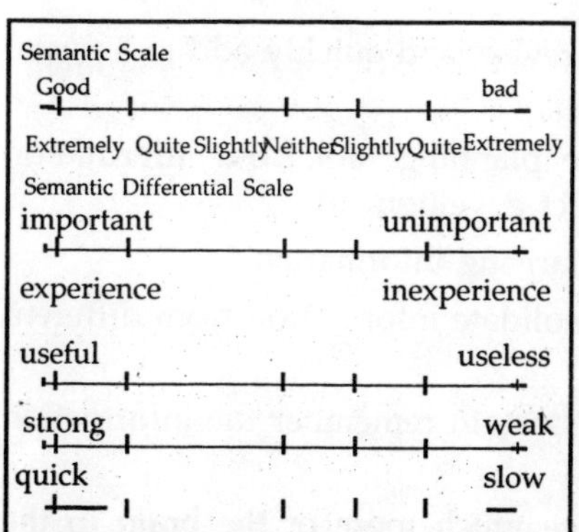 *Likhert Scale*	*Scale* This strategy uses a scale that allows students or groups being surveyed to indicate to what extent they agree or disagree with a statement, attitude or problem. To ensure thoughtful responses are given it is necessary to frame statements in such a way that both ends of the rating scale are used.

through cognitive development; they rely mainly on language skills. The first ingredient of learning is comprehension. Concept development and language are integral parts of the child's overall cognitive development.

Graphic organisers

1. make content area information more accessible to learners.
2. convert complex information into manageable chunks.
3. help students develop higher level thinking skills and promote creativity.
4. encourage students to think about information in new ways.
5. it helps in transfer of learning -with graphic organisers, the students focus on the connections instead of the words.
6. are effective tools in activities that ask students to revise and recapitulate concepts and demonstrate their understanding especially in seminars for students in higher classes and university population.
7. help students think clearly and creatively
8. enable students to adapt or make changes
9. help learners to think perspectively or to think from different angles..
10. help the students to gain the 'entire view' or 'big view' of the topic; students gain insightful learning or whole-picture learning
11. these are easy to edit, revise, and quickly add to a visual map.
12. can be used as a nice planning tool from information identification to product development.
13. help learners in summarising information
14. enable learners to consolidate information from different research sources
15. provide the cues necessary to remember the information within it.
16. help learners to engage much more of the brain in the process of assimilating and connecting facts than conventional notes.

17. are used to stimulate idea generation and are used for brain-storming.
18. can also be seen as a first step in ontology-building, and can also be used flexibly to represent formal argument.
19. are widely used in education for note taking and summarizing
20. help learners elicit knowledge for individual expert knowledge and team knowledge.
21. enable learners in gleaning key concepts, their relationships and hierarchy from documents and source materials.
22. are used mainly in transforming tacit knowledge into an visual explicit organisational resource and knowledge.
23. help in facilitating the creation of shared vision and shared understanding within a team or organisation.
24. are used in communicating complex ideas and arguments:
25. help to exxamine the symmetry of complex ideas and arguments and associated terminology.
26. help learners to apply think-aloud strategies to aid in meta-cognition and verbalise their thinking - enhancing metacognition (learning to learn, and thinking about knowledge)
27. enable learners to preview text to generate questions and answers, stimulate prior knowledge, make predictions, and interact with print
28. provide self-monitoring and self-correct strategies to aid in conceptual understanding of content material
29. use summarisation strategies to identify, process, and comprehend crucial information in a text
30. help learners to discuss material with peers, monitor and correct their own work, encourage and support one another, and reinforce social skills in collaborative learning groups.
31. promote organisation of text, whether it be in reading or writing.
32. serve as templates to help readers dissect information.

33. incorporate signaling techniques or fit predetermined, common modalities of text paganisaion/structure.
34. can be used as tools for structuring information, of arranging important aspects of a concept or topic into a pattern using labels..
35. provide learners a focal point – as learners read and think about what they have read, graphic organisers give students an easy way to organise their thoughts.
36. can be incorporated into teaching students of all ability levels - to teach problem-solving skills and to teach reading skills helpful for comprehending mathematics, social studies, language, history and science or any other subject.
37. can help students with historical inquiry and result in improved thinking skills, more sophisticated conclusions and better decision making.
38. speed up communication because visual symbols are quickly and easily recognised.
39. help people organise, remember and recall information. They explain complex relationships among elements with a minimum use of text
40. they can help clarify concepts that cannot be communicated through words.
41. help students create their own concept maps and thus fosters a meta-cognitive awareness of how they are making meaning and encourages them to be more aware of how their understanding of a concept changes as new ideas are added and reviewed by reading more text or participating in discussion.

9

Semantic Networks

Chapter Overview

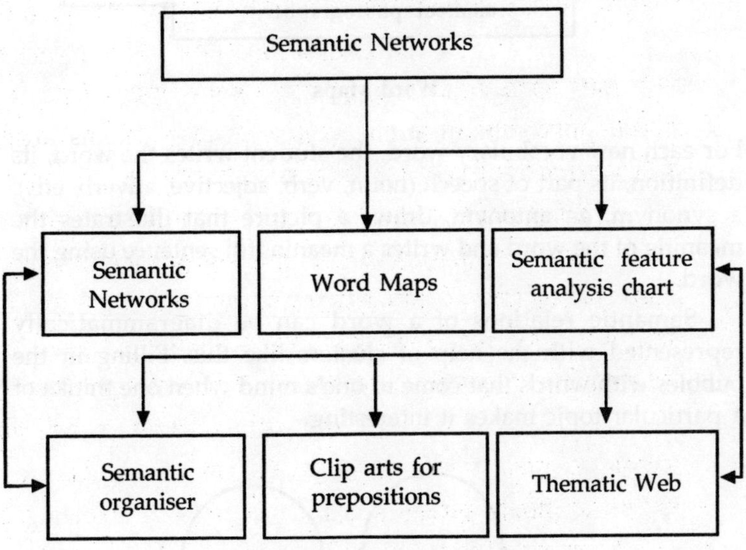

Semantic Network

A semantic network is a way of representing relationships between concepts. Often each concept is represented by a word or set of words.

For example one can create a semantic network for the word 'amateur' as given in the following diagram.

Vocabulary maps are graphic organisers that can be useful in helping a student learn new vocabulary words.

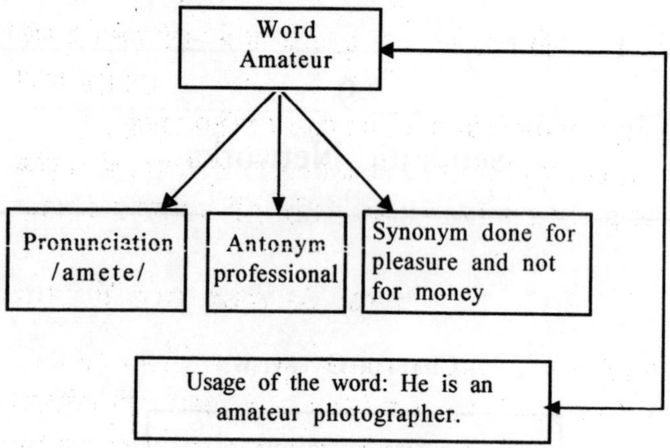

Word Maps

For each new vocabulary word, the student writes the word, its definition, its part of speech (noun, verb, adjective, adverb, etc.), a synonym, an antonym, draws a picture that illustrates the meaning of the word and writes a meaningful sentence using the word.

Semantic relations of a word can be diagrammatically represented with the help of clusters like this. Filling in the bubbles with words that come to one's mind when one thinks of a particular topic makes it interesting.

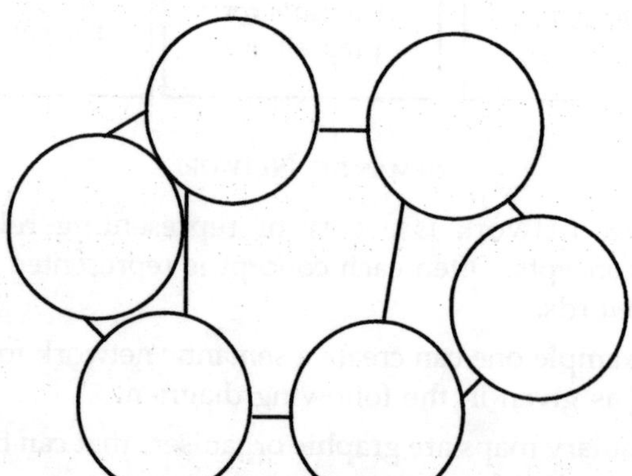

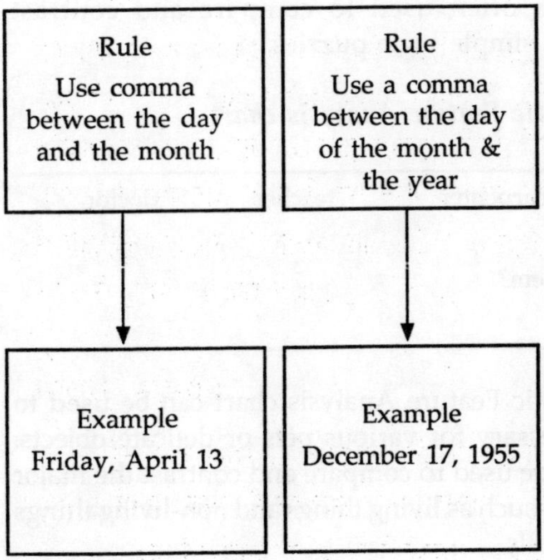

How to use commas in written English can be demonstrated with 'Rule' and 'Example' as given below:

Commas in Addresses

1. Use a comma between the city and State or country
2. If an address is given in the middle of a sentence, set off the address with commas

> Chennai, Tamilnadu
> Mumbai, India

> We shifted to 239, T.V.Samy Rd, R.S.Puram, Coimbatore, last month.

Semantic Feature Analysis Chart Diagrams

Semantic Feature Analysis charts are used to examine the similarities and differences of a group of items, people, events etc.

This type of chart is often used to compare and contrast characteristics and for simple logic puzzles.

Semantic Feature Analysis chart

Description	carpenter	teacher	doctor
What work do they do?			
How do you describe them?			
Where do they work?			

For example, a Semantic Feature Analysis chart can be used to compare the care necessary for various pets or delicate objects. This type of chart can be used to compare and contrast the major features of any concept-such as living things and non-living things or plant and animal cells.

Semantic Organiser

This organiser asks students to categorise a collection of words.

Fill in the details in the following table:

Word	*Meaning*	*Part of Speech*	*Derivatives*
Explore			
Adventure			
Astronomy			
Gravity			
Universe			

Create a semantic network by writing the 'pronunciation', 'synonyms' and 'antonyms' for the following words and using them in sentences of your own.

daring
tragic
knowledge
eager
risky

Cliparts and graphics can be used to portray and teach grammar and vocabulary. Here is an example for teaching preposition indicating movement and time.

Preposition of Movement

Picture It Clip Art	*Preposition*	*Example*
	To	"He carried the rubbish to the bin."
	Through	"The train came through the tunnel."
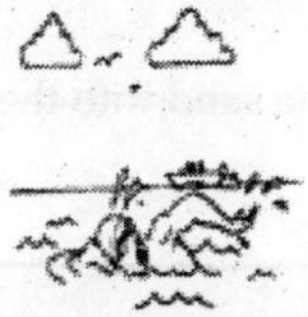	Across	"He swam across the channel."
	Along	"He walked along the road."
	Down	"He skied down the mountain."

(Contd...)

(Contd...)

Picture It Clip Art	*Preposition*	*Example*
	Over	“They walked over the bridge.”
	Off	“The man ran off the cliff.”
	Round ball.”	“The arrow is moving round the
	Into	“The man poured the sand into the timer.

Preposition of Time

Picture It Clip Art	*Preposition*	
	at (a time)	“I got to work at 8.00 this morning.”
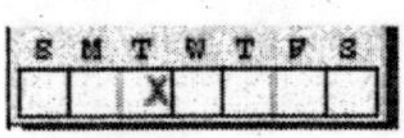	on (a day)	“I'll see you on Tuesday.”
	on (a date)	“I have an appointment on the 31st.”

(Contd...)

Picture It Clip Art	*Preposition*	
	in (a month)	"My birthday is in June"
	in (a year)	"I was born in 1959"
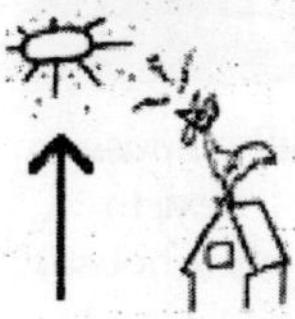	in (the morning)	"I get up in the morning."
	in (the afternoon)	"I have lunch in the afternoon."
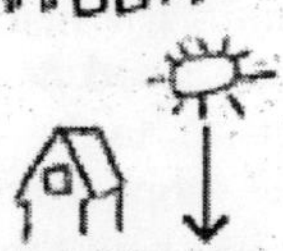	in (the evening)	"I go home in the evening."
	at (night)	"I go to bed at night."
	in (a season)	"It usually snows in the winter."

Preposition of Place

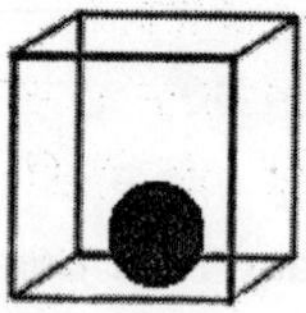

The ball is in the box

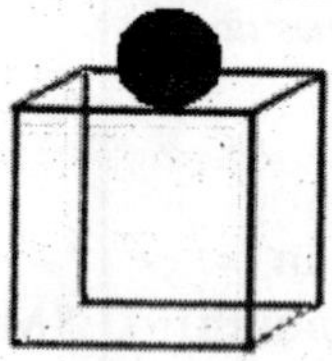

The ball is on the box.

The ball is under the box.

John's house

John's house is next to Jane's house.

Jane's house

Jane's house is between Bill's and John's houses.

Bill's house

Bill's house is next to Jane's house.

The climbers stood on top of the mountain.

The man stood between the two enemies.

The enemies stood opposite each other.

The gardners stood behind the pumpkins.

The man stood next to the gopher and held the umbrella over it.

The man looked through the telescope in his hands.

The man wrote the address on the package.

The man looked at the mail in the post box.

The man looked at the clock on the wall.

The manager sat at his desk on his chair

Bridge Map for Analogies

Animal	Baby
Dog	puppy
Cat	?
Cow	calf
Goat	?

This kind of mapping skill helps learners to extrapolate or interpolate, use proper vocabulary to describe and to recognise relationships.

Schema (pl. schemata) – A schema is a hierarchic network of internalised knowledge. For example, a schema about "restaurants" might include choosing which restaurant to go to, being seated by a table, being given a menu, ordering food, eating, paying the bill, etc.

Thematic Web

Thematic web is a technique for organising instruction around a central theme. Thematic webs enable the planner to extend the

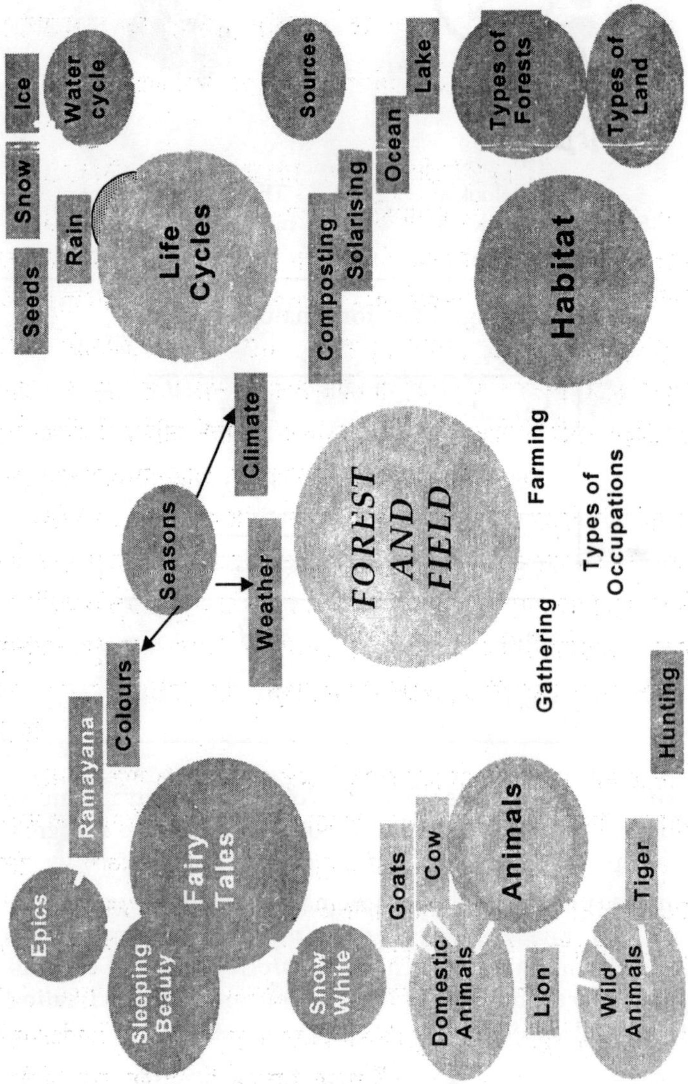

Thematic Web

theme in various directions and organising the topic in meaningful categories. Suppose the lesson deals with 'Forests and Fields', creating this type of thematic web will enable the learners to get the complete picture of the topic. It enables the teacher to build up the subject matter further and discuss all issues related to the topic. The topic can be extended and expanded to any level and several dimensions can be added to the topic to make it more enriching.

Adjectives and Adverbs

Adjectives and adverbs can be easily taught to students with Learning Disabilities, Hearing Impairment and ADHD and Slow learners easily with the help of these diagrams which are used under 'Brainstorming' techniques.

The explanation can be highlighted by enclosing it in a box or in a photo frame as in the following examples.

> **Adjectives**
>
> Adjectives modify nouns and pronouns and answer the following questions - Which one?, What kind?, How many?.
> They may be words, phrases or clauses

> **Adverbs**
>
> Adverbs modify verbs, adjectives or other adverbs and answer the questions *where?*, *why?*, *when?* and *how?* Most words ending in —ly are adverbs.

The example given here does not demand much of the students. These diagrams not only clarify the meaning and assist pupils in their practice of the use of grammatical points but also draw the pupils' attention to the precise form of the language.

Using Mapping Skills for Teaching Grammar

Grammar is often misunderstood in the language teaching field. The misconception lies in the view that grammar is a collection of arbitrary rules about static structures in the language. Further questionable claims are that the structures do not have to be taught, learners will acquire them on their own, or if the structures are taught, the lessons that ensue will be boring. Consequently, communicative and proficiency-based teaching approaches sometimes unduly limit grammar instruction.

But a teacher of English Grammar knows well the significance of the parts of speech - Noun, Adjective, Pronoun, Verb, Adverb, Preposition, Conjunction and Interjection. It is imperative that the learners master the skill in using these parts of speech correctly in order that rephrasing, précis, expanding, transformation of one kind of sentence into other forms like Voice, Degrees of comparison and Simple- Compound- Complex are rendered easier thus enhancing better communication in speech and writing. Practical English rules are still being obeyed especially in academic writing. Also grammar is a sure ground of reference when linguistic habits fail us.

But the kind of exercises given for identification often are watertight compartments and the students still grope in the dark and stay clueless. Grammar has gained bad reputation because often it has been taught as a separate skill strangely dissociated from the rest of language learning. It is not been fun; it is not meaningful. Thus grammar is a word that freezes the heart of students and teachers alike. So teaching English grammar has taken a retreat and often, not a palatable one and this has given room to many myths. Some of these myths are

1. Grammar is acquired naturally; it need not be taught
2. Grammar is a collection of meaningless forms.
3. Grammar consists of arbitrary rules.
4. Grammar is boring.
5. Students have different learning styles. Not all students can learn grammar.

If the goals of language instruction include teaching students to use grammar accurately, meaningfully, and appropriately, then a compelling case can be made for teaching grammar. Instead of viewing grammar as a static system of arbitrary rules, it should be seen as a rational, dynamic system that is comprised of structures characterized by the three dimensions of form, meaning, and use. So the aim of this Action Research is to make our pupils skilled enough to use grammar in an unselfconscious fashion to achieve their communicative ends. If the concept of learning the parts of speech through steps is internalized, the writer feels that the myths will no more be the stumbling blocks to master grammar.

So the writer being a teacher of English earlier and now a teacher educator, has come up with a simpler technique. It is called Learning Grammar through Steps. Instead of following the conventional spilt - up of sentences, the writer has clubbed the allied parts of speech to enable the learner to work with ease. Thus Adjectives, Nouns and Pronouns form the first category and Verbs and Adverbs another group. As Conjunctions join the clauses, they occupy the middle column. Preposition comes next followed by Interjection.

The writer, as a teacher of English, had tried this strategy with her pupils as an Action Research and found it a phenomenal success. The technique is described in steps with their advantages.

Pre – Requisite or Spade Work for this Programme

It is imperative that the pupils are taught the usage of the parts of speech before they proceed to work out this strategy.

Steo 1 - Selecting a running passage

Advantages

When the exercises given for identification has sentences arranged one after the other, each sentence may appear as an isolated unit. But when the sentences are in a running passage, continuity of thought and cogency of matter is maintained thus enhancing better involvement on the part of the learner, even the late bloomer to begin work with ease.

The passage is selected according to the age group / difficulty level of the pupils. The writer has given a simple passage as an example.

Passage

One sunny spring day Mr. Johnson sat fishing. Near him on the lake many wild ducks were swimming. Mr. Johnson liked to watch the birds get their food; he liked to watch them spring into the fresh morning open air. Down went their bills into the mud of the lake. Up went their tails. How funny they looked!

The ducks, all at once rose into the air. Together they flew up the lake as if they were having a race. They dived into the lake suddenly. What a splash they made!

Step 2- Reading the passage

Students read the passage well. This followed by the teacher's reading with expression, stress and intonation. Here, to enhance better understanding of the passage the teacher can make use of suitable visuals.

Advantages

Reading the passage well enhances better comprehension.

Step -3 Splitting the passage in to individual sentences

Advantages

We need a running passage to start with but that format has to be broken into sentences so that the parts of speech are identified and marked with comfortable ease. The learners also know a running passage has sentences of varying lengths. They also, by practice, internalize the rule of demarking a sentence-*it begins with a capital and ends with a fullstop.*

Passage Split into Sentences

1. One sunny spring day Mr. Johnson sat fishing.
2. Near him on the lake many wild ducks were swimming.
3. Mr. Johnson liked to watch them get their food; he also liked to watch them spring into the fresh morning open air
4. Down went their bills into the mud of the lake.
5. Up went their tails.

6. How funny they looked!
7. The ducks, all at once rose into the air.
8. Together they flew up the lake as if they were having a race.
9. They dived into the lake suddenly.
10. What a splash they made!

Step 3 Drawing a table with the columns

S.No	*Adjective*	*Noun*	*Pro-noun*	*Con-junction*	*Pre-position*	*Verb*	*Adverb*	*Inter-jection*
1.								
2.								
3.								
4.								
5.								
6.								
7.								
8.								
9.								
10.								

Step 4 Picking out the parts of speech

Pupils are encouraged mark one part of speech eg: noun in all the sentences:

i) Pupils pick the nouns first – Name words are easy to start with

ii) Then they proceed to look for the adjectives, the qualifiers for nouns. This is easy as the adjectives, most often, precede the nouns.

iii) Next the pupils pick the pronouns as the pronouns stand for the nouns.

iv) Now the pupils pick the verbs.

v) Based on the verbs, the adverbs, the qualifiers of verbs are picked.

vi) Next the prepositions,

vii) The conjunctions

viii) And lastly the interjections are marked.

Advantages of this Technique

— When the same parts of speech are repeated in a running passage, the pupils get a reinforcement of the concepts.

— Pupils know a same word can be used to mean different parts of speech. E.g. 'spring' as Noun and as Verb. (Sentence - 3)

— The pupils also know that each sentence has a Finite Verb, even if other parts of speech are missing.

— The pupils also realized that in running passage there are a very few Interjections.

— The pupils learn that the Adverbs occupy the initial or the middle or the final position in a sentence.

Example

Initials position - sentences 2,4,5 and 8.

Middle position - sentences 3 and 7.

Final position - sentences 9.

— The pupils learn that the Articles (a, an, the)are adjectives, as they qualify nouns.

— The pupils learn that more than one adjectives can be used to describe a noun. (Sentence – 1, 2, 3)

Table 1 - With Nouns

S. No.	Adj.	Noun	Pro.	Con.	Pre.	Ver.	Adv.	Int.
I.		day						
		Mr. Johnson						
2.		lake						
		ducks						
3.		Mr. Johnson						
		food						
		air						
4.		bills						
		mud						
		lake						
5.		tails						
6.		—						
7.		ducks						
		air						
8.		lake						
		race						
9.		lake						
10.		splash						

Table 2 - Nouns and Adjectives

S. No.	*Adj.*	*Nou.*	*Pro.*	*Con.*	*Pre.*	*Ver.*	*Adv.*	*Int.*
1.	One sunny spring	day						
		Mr. Johnson						
2.	the							
	many wild	lake						
		ducks						
3.		Mr. Johnson						
	their	food,						
	the fresh morning open	air						
4.	their	bills						
	the	mud						
	the	lake						
5.	their	tails						
6.	—	—						
7.	The	ducks						
	the	air						
8.	the	lake						
	a	race						
9.	the	lake						
10.	a	splash						

Table 3 — With Nouns, Adjectives and Pronouns

S. No.	*Adj.*	*Nou.*	*Pro.*	*Con.*	*Pre.*	*Ver.*	*Adv.*	*Int.*
1.	One sunny spring	day						
		Mr. Johnson	—					
2.	the	lake						
	many wild	ducks	him					
3.		Mr. Johnson	he					
	their	food	them					
	the fresh morning open	air	them					
4.	their	bills						
	the	mud						
	the	lake	—					
5.	their	tails	—					
6.	—	—	they					
7.	The	ducks						
	the	air	—					
8.	the	lake	they					
	a	race	they					
9.	the	lake	they					
10.	a	splash	they					

Table 4 : With Nouns, Adjectives, Pronouns and Verbs

S. No.	*Adj.*	*Nou.*	*Pro.*	*Con.*	*Pre.*	*Ver.*	*Adv.*	*Int.*
1.	One sunny spring	day						
		Mr. Johnson	—			sat^{fv} fishing^{ifv}		
2.	the	lake						
	many wild	ducks	him			were swimming^{ifv}		
3.		Mr. Johnson	he			liked^{fv} to watch^{ifv}		
	their	food	them			get^{fv}		
	the fresh morning open	air	them			spring^{ifv}		
						liked^{fv} to watch^{fv}		
4.	their	bills	—			went^{fv}		
	the	mud						
	the	lake						
5.	their	tails	—			went^{fv}		
6.	—	—	they			looked^{fv}		
7.	The	ducks						
		air	—			rose^{fv}		
8.	the	lake	they			flew^{fv}		
	a	race	they			were having^{fv}		
9.	the	lake	they			dived^{fv}		
10.	a	splash	they			made^{fv}		

fv = Finite verb; ifv = infinite verbs (fishing = participle (sentence 1), to watch = infinite(sentence 3) get = bare infinite verb (sentence 3)

Table 5 : With Nouns Adjectives Pronouns Verbs and Adverbs

S. No.	*Adj.*	*Nou.*	*Pro.*	*Con.*	*Pre.*	*Ver.*	*Adv.*	*Int.*
1.	One sunny spring	day						
		Mr. Johnson	—			satfv fishingfv	—	
2.	the	lake					Near	
	many wild	ducks	Him			were swimmingfv		
3.		Mr. Johnson	He			liked^{fv} to watch^{ifv}		
	their	food	them			get^{fv}		
	the fresh morning open	air	them			spring^{ifv}		
						liked^{fv} to watch^{fv}	also	
4.	their	bills	—			went^{fv}	Down	
	the	mud						
	the	lake						
5.	their	tails	—			went^{fv}	Up	
6.	—	—	They			looked^{fv}	funny	
7.	The	ducks						
		air	—			rose^{fv}	all at once	
8.	the	lake	They			flew^{fv}	up	
	a	race	They			were having^{fv}	Together	
9.	the	lake	They			dived^{fv}	suddenly	
10.	a	splash	They			made!^{fv}		

fv = Finite verb; ifv = infinite verbs (fishing = participle (sentence 1), to watch = infinite(sentence 3) get = bare infinite verb (sentence 3)

Table 6: With Nouns, Adjectives, Pronouns, Verbs, Adverbs and Prepositions

S. No.	Adj.	Nou.	Pro.	Con.	Pre.	Ver.	Adv. Int.
1.	One sunny spring	day					
		Mr. Johnson	—		—	sat^{fv} fishing^{ifv}	—
2.	the	lake			on		Near
	many wild	ducks	Him			were swimming^{fv}	
3.							
	their	Mr. Johnson	He		—	liked^{fv} to watch^{ifv}	
	the fresh morning open	food	them			get^{fv}	
		air	them		into	spring^{ifv}	
						liked^{fv} to watch^{fv}	also
4.	their	bills	—			went^{fv}	Down
	the	mud			into		
	the	lake			of		
5.	their	tails	—			went^{fv}	Up
6.	—	—	They			looked!^{fv}	funny
7.	The	ducks	—		into	rose^{fv}	all at once
t	he	air					
8.	the	lake	They		—	flew^{fv}	up
	a	race	They			were having^{fv}	Together
9.	the	lake	They		into	dived^{fv}	suddenly
10.	a	splash	They			made!^{fv}	

fv = Finite verb; ifv = infinite verbs (fishing = participle (sentence 1), to watch = infinite(sentence 3) get = bare infinite verb (sentence 3)

Table 7 : With Nouns, Adjectives, Pronouns, Verbs, Adverbs, Prepositions and Interjections

S. No.	Adj.	Nou.	Pro.	Con.	Pre.	Ver.	Adv.	Int.
1.	One sunny spring	day						
		Mr. Johnson	-	-	-	sat^{fv} fishing^{ifv}	-	-
2.	the	lake			on			Near
	many wild	ducks	Him	-		were swimming^{fv}		
3.								
	their	Mr. Johnson	He			liked^{fv} to watch^{ifv}		
	the fresh morning open	food	them			get^{ifv}		
		air	them		into	spring^{ifv}		
						likedfv to watch^{ifv}		also
4.	their	bills	—	—	into	went^{fv}		Down
	the	mud			of			
	the	lake	-	-				
5.	their	tails	-	-	-	went^{fv}	Up	-
6.	-	-	They	-	-	looked!^{fv}	funny	How
7.	The	ducks			into	rose^{fv}	all at once	-
	the	air						
8.	the	lake	They			flew^{fv}	up	
	a	race	They	as if		were having^{fv}	Together	
9.	the	lake	They	-	into	dived^{fv}	suddenly	-
10.	a	splash	They			made!^{fv}		What

fv = Finite verb; ifv = infinite verbs (fishing = participle (sentence 1), to watch = infinite(sentence 3) get = bare infinite verb (sentence 3)

The Complete Table 8 : With Nouns, Adjectives, Pronouns, Verbs, Adverbs Prepositions and Conjunctions

S. No.	*Adj.*	*Nou.*	*Pro.*	*Con.*	*Pre.*	*Ver.*	*Adv.*	*Int.*
1.	One sunny spring	day						
		Mr. Johnson	–	–	–	satfv fishing^{ifv}	–	–
2.	the	lake						
	many wild	ducks	Him	–	on	were swimming^{fv}	Near	–
3.		Mr. Johnson	He			likedfv to watch^{ifv}		
	their	food	them			get^{ifv}		
	the fresh morning open	air	them	–	into	spring^{ifv}		
						likedfv to watch^{ifv}	also	
4.	their	bills	–	–	into	went^{fv}	Down	
	the	mud			of.			
	the	lake						
5.	their	tails	–	–	–	went^{fv}	Up	–
6.	–	–	They	–	–	looked!^{fv}	funny	How
7.	The	ducks						
	the	air	–	–	into	rose^{fv}	all at once	–
8.	the	lake	They		—	flew^{fv}	up	
	a	race	They	as if		were having^{fv}	Together	
9.	the	lake	They	–	into	dived^{fv}	suddenly	–
10.	A	splash	They			made^{fv}		What

fv = Finite verb;

ifv = infinite verbs (fishing = participle (sentence 1), to watch = infinite (sentence 3) get & spring = bare infinite verb (sentence 3)

Once the pupils get a firm footing regarding the parts of speech, the teacher can help them with the advanced steps. (Source: T.K. Satyakumari's paper entitled 'Grammar through steps– the easy way !')

10

Mathematical Signs as Graphic Organisers

Chapter Overview

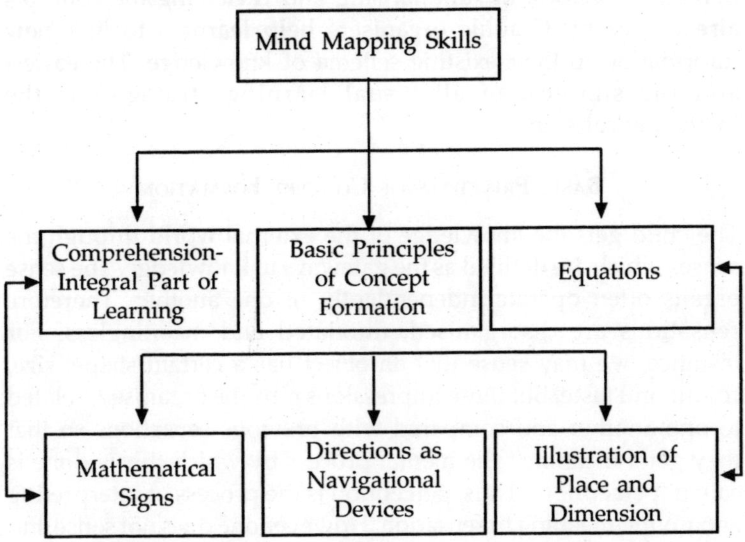

Comprehension: An Integral Part of Learning

The classroom teacher's major responsibility in a class is to understand how children learn. Many psychologists are of the opinion that children move through a series of progressive stages of development in which differentiation becomes more and more refined, flexibility increases and knowledge expands. The child moves from simple to more complex levels of concept development and thinking. The ability to comprehend is an integral part of any learning. Comprehension acts as a bridge between the known and the unknown.

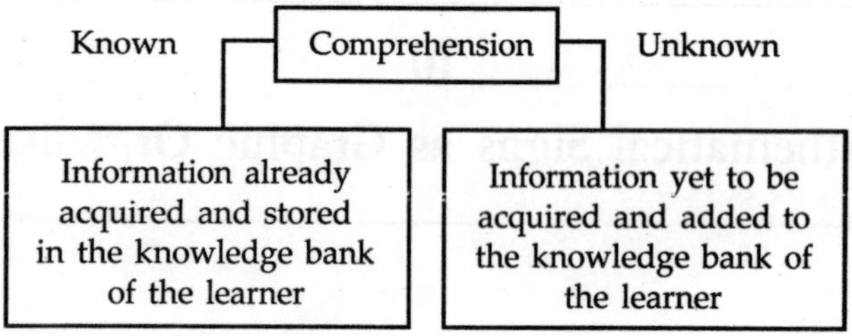

Graphic organisers assist students in the note-taking and note-making processes, in summarising and reviewing the concepts already learnt. Graphic organisers help learners to link new information to their existing schema of knowledge. The easiest and the simplest of all visual learning strategies is the mathematical sign.

Basic Principles of Concept Formation

The child gets the knowledge of the external world through the senses which are defined as the gateways to knowledge. The sense organs often operate independently of one another. Therefore sensations are disorganised, unrelated and meaningless. For instance, we may sense that an object has a certain shape, size, colour and taste. But these impressions must be organised, related to one another and compared with previous sensations so that they get a meaning. The mental process by which this is done is called 'perception'. Thus, perception is the process of interpreting and giving meaning to sensation. However one does not sense and then perceive. Both the processes go together. The process of perception results in the formation of percepts that are simply organisation of sensory experiences about a particular object. These percepts are the basis for the formation of concepts. Thus sensation and perception are two stages that lead to concept-formation.

Equations

The entire paragraph can be simply illustrated with an equation like this:

Sensation + meaning = Perception

Perception + generalisation = Concept formation

MATHEMATICAL SIGNS AS GRAPHIC ORGANISERS

Using mathematical signs such as +, -, and = several concepts can be taught to children. Synonyms are words that have same or similar meaning. Synonyms are taught using the mathematical sign for 'equals' as in the following example:

aid	=	help	domicile	=	place of residence
fierce	=	savage	misery	=	sorrow

Antonyms are words that are opposites. For example, 'sad' is the antonym of the word 'happy'.

The mathematical sign that is used to indicate the opposite of something is X. Words that are opposites in meaning can be taught in this way:

ancient	X	modern	rich	X	poor	tall	X	short
full	X	empty	high	X	low	clean	X	dirty

In order to describe suffix, we can use the mathematical signs. A suffix is an ending that is added to a word. Some suffixes can be added to words to form nouns. For example:

word + suffix = noun

teach + er = teacher

Other mathematical symbols can be used to illustrate for example 'prepositions'. A preposition expresses a relation between two entities. Of the various types of relational meaning those of PLACE and TIME are the most prominent and easy to identify. For instance, prepositions such as above, over, on top of, under, underneath, beneath, below express relative position vertically whereas before, in front of, behind, after represent it horizontally. All these prepositions can be easily taught with the help of a diagram or mathematical sign like this. (Courtesy: *A University Grammar of English* by Quirk & Greenbaum, (1973). Longman Group Limited. pp. 148-151).

Directions as Navigational Devices

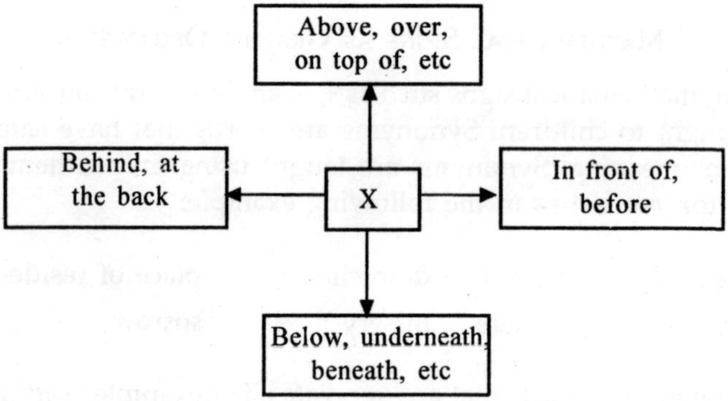

Direction

Up, down, along, across, around that express motion or movement with reference to an axis or directional path can be explained through a graphic like this. Over and under as place prepositions are roughly synonymous with above and below respectively.

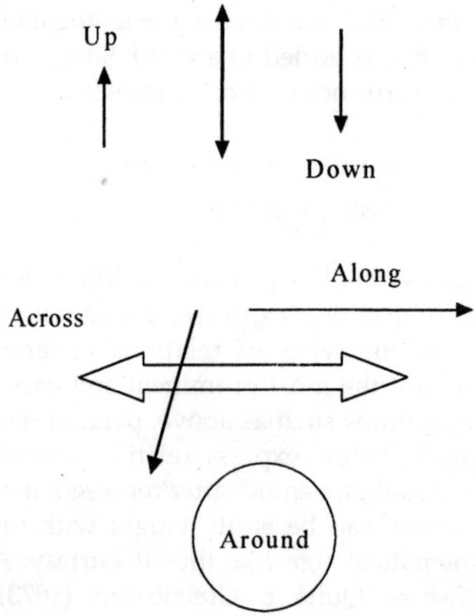

Up and down contrast in terms of vertical direction, while along (from one end towards the other) and across (from one side to another) in terms of a horizontal axis. But up and down are also used idiomatically in reference to a horizontal axis.

For example

'I walked up and down the platform'.

Up and down here express the notion of along and need not have any vertical implications. With round the directional path is an angle or a curve:

'We ran up the hill'.

'We ran round the corner'.

In order to teach combinations of colours, the mathematical sign of '+' can be effectively used as in:

There are three primary colours for mixing paints or pigments.

Yellow + red = orange

Yellow + blue = green

Blue + red = purple

Blue + red + green = black .

Place and dimension can be best illustrated with the following table.

Place & Dimension	*Positive Direction*	*Positive Position*	*Negative Direction*	*Negative Position*
Dimension (Point)	to	at	Away or from	Away or from

Dimension (line or surface)	On (to)	On	Off	Off
	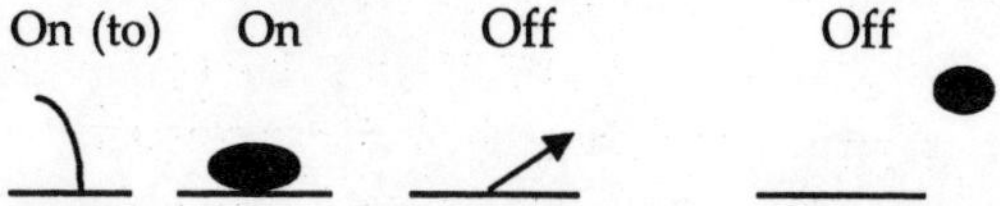			
Dimension (area or volume	In (to)	in	Out of	Out of
	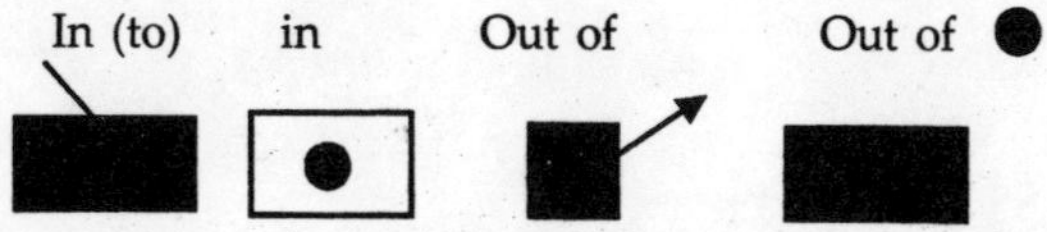			

Thus mathematical signs and symbols can be used to express various concepts effectively.

11
Sequential Graphic Organisers

Chapter Overview

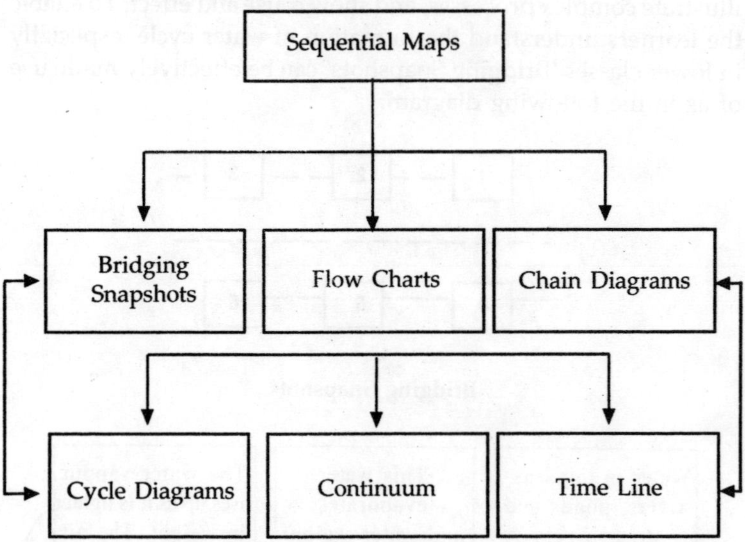

Sequential graphic organisers represent serial information. Timelines represent information that proceeds in temporal order. Flowcharts represent information that is also serial, but there are discrete steps, or steps that must be completed in order. When all the steps in a flowchart are dependent on the previous one, and when the last step is connected to the first step, then a cyclical organiser is best. A hierarchy is also like a flowchart, except each subordinate step may have more than one branch. Sequencing graphics are used to describe the stages of something (the life cycle of a primate, a frog or a butterfly or watercycle); the steps in a linear procedure (how to neutralise an acid); a sequence of events (how Sepoy mutiny led to Indian War of Independence); or the goals, actions, and outcomes of a historical figure or character in a novel (the rise and fall of Hitler); sequencing is used when prioritising elements from most important to least important; relative position or standing; a series of things or persons; or an orderly arrangement from first to last.

Bridging Snapshots

Sequencing charts such as Bridging Snapshots are used to portray changes over time, reveal the sequence of step-by-step methods, illustrate complex processes, and show cause and effect. To enable the learners understand the formation of water cycle, especially in lower classes 'Bridging Snapshots' can be effectively made use of as in the following diagram.

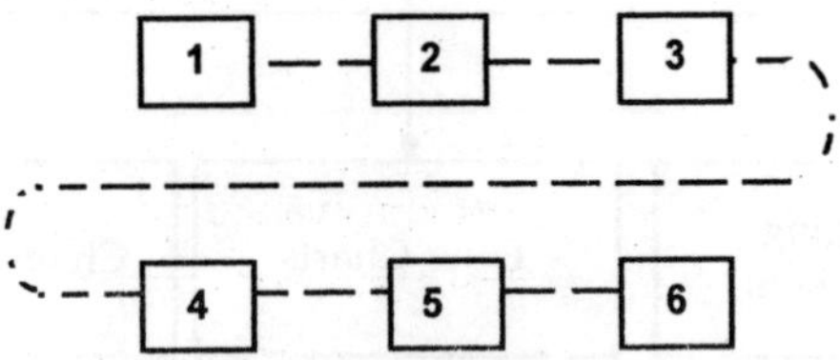

Bridging Snapshots

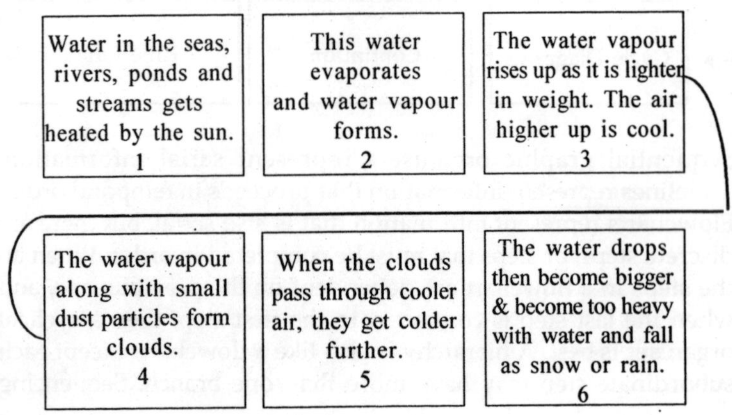

This process is repeated over and over again and thus the 'Water Cycle' in nature goes on and on.

FLOWCHARTS

Objectives of a Flowchart

a) A flowchart illustrates the steps in a process. By visualising the process, a flowchart can quickly help identify bottlenecks or inefficiencies where the process can be streamlined or improved.

b) A drawing that uses symbols interconnected with lines to represent the flow of information.

c) A process flow diagram illustrates the successive steps in a process, procedure, system or model.

Basic Flowcharting Shapes

Flowcharts use special shapes to represent different types of actions or steps in a process. Lines and arrows show the sequence of the steps, and the relationships among them.

Concept Flowcharting (Concept Mapping)

This involves creating a flow model that contains a concept, item or question for exploring knowledge, new information, new ideas, or relationships; to illustrate an individual's concept of knowledge in a specific area or to communicate complex ideas. The various maps or models are: Concept Diagram, Concept Map, Concept Model, Concept Module, Concept Flowchart, Conceptual Map or Conceptual Model.

Information Knowledge Mapping (Mind Mapping)

Similar to a concept map, it involves creating a flow model that explores knowledge, new information, new ideas, or relationships; an illustration of one's knowledge in a specific area; or a model that communicates complex ideas. The various maps or models are: Information Map or Information Flow Model, Mind Map, Inspiration Diagram, Brainstorm Map, Circle Map, Bubble Map, Thinking Map or Thought Map.

Organisation of flowcharts Using Colors

One of the goals of concept mapping or mind mapping is to create connected groups of subtopics and to create hierarchy between ideas.

To help differentiate between related groups of subtopics, one can mark them with different colours. Colour and shape of the flowcharts can be changed by first selecting it and then choosing from the colour palettes in the Shapes and Lines menus. The fill colour, shading, border colour, border thickness, border style, line colour, line thickness, can be changed as per requirements.

Flowcharts, also called sequence of events diagrams, are a type of graphic organisers that describe the stages or steps in a process; they visually display a chain of instructions used to complete an algorithm or other complicated process.

Symbols Used in Flowcharts	Meanings
	Direction of Flow
	Starting, stopping or Control Point
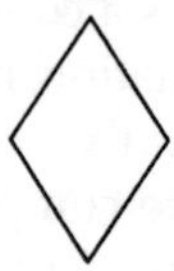	Decision Point
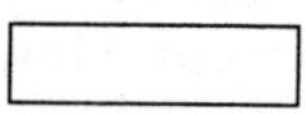	Processing takes place
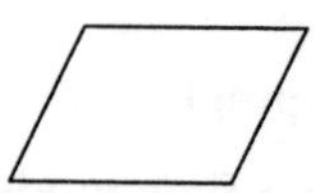	Input or output

Flowcharts have a beginning, multiple possible outcomes at some nodes, rules at some nodes, and possible multiple endings. In flowcharts, different symbols have different meanings.

a) Arrows represent the direction of flow.

b) Circles and ovals for starting, stopping, or control points.

c) Diamonds are decision points.

d) Rectangles and squares are steps at which processing takes place.

e) Parallelograms represent input or output.

For example, computer programmers use flowcharts to organise an algorithm before writing a programme.

What is the object, procedure, or initiating event?

What triggered the event?

What are the stages or steps?

How do they lead to one another?

What is the final outcome?

The student must be able to identify the first step in the process, all of the resulting stages in the procedure as they unfold, and the outcome (the final stage). In this process, the student realizes how one step leads to the next in the process, and eventually, to the outcome.

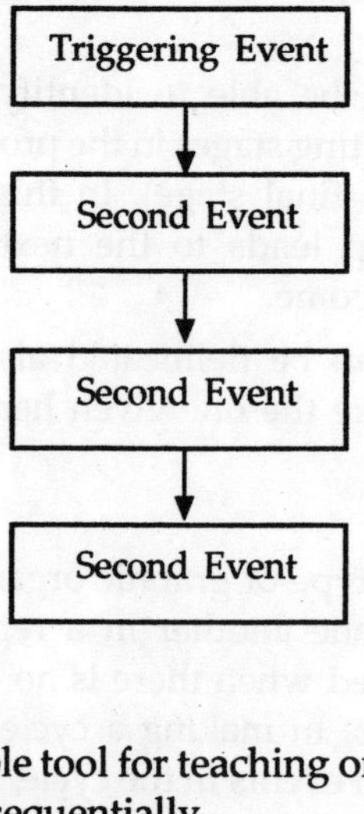

Train of Thoughts

This is a very serviceable tool for teaching or learning any concept that can be arranged sequentially.

At primary level, this picture can be used to depict various concepts. Each coach or bogie of the train may represent a dimension or a characteristic and each coach can be numbered also.

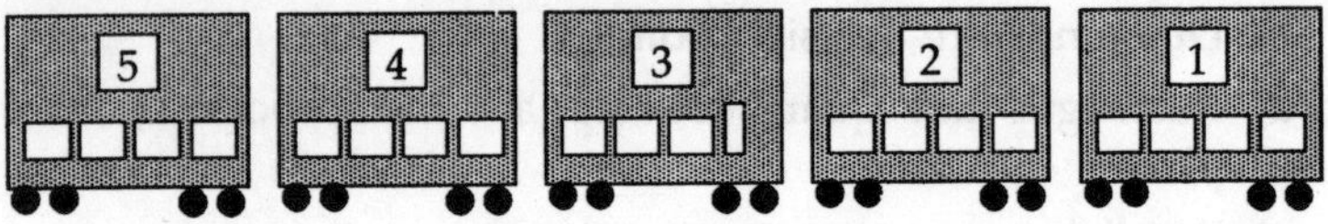

1. Bacteria and other microbes or micro-organisms rot down
2. Recycle nutrients in the soil.
3. These nutrients are absorbed by plants.
4. The plants in turn provide food for animals.
5. Dead animals and other wastes decay and enrich the soil by providing nutrients to the soil and the cycle continues.

Chain Diagrams

Chain diagrams, also called sequence of events diagrams, are a type of graphic organisers that describe the stages or steps in a process or the stages of an event, the actions of character or the steps in a procedure. Chain diagrams are useful in examining linear cause-and-effect processes and other processes that unfold sequentially.

The student must be able to identify the first step in the process, all of the resulting stages in the procedure as they unfold, and the outcome (the final stage). In this process, the student realises how one step leads to the next in the process, and eventually, to the outcome.

The watercycle can be delineated also with the help of a 'sequence diagram' like the one given here. (see on next page)

Cycle

Cycle diagrams are a type of graphic organisers that shows how items are related to one another in a repeating cycle. A cycle diagram is usually used when there is no beginning and no end to a repeating process. In making a cycle diagram, the student must identify the main events in the cycle, how they interact, and how the cycle repeats.

A depiction of a cycle attempts to show how a series of events interacts to produce a set of results again and again such as the lifecycle of an organism.

Chain Diagrams

Insects like butterflies and moths undergo four stages in their life and this is called their life cycle or metamorphosis. Metamorphosis is the growth of an insect – from egg to adult. The four stages of the butterfly are

1. Egg Stage
2. Larva Stage
3. Pupa Stage
4. Adult Stage

This can be better explained with the 'Cycle' diagram.

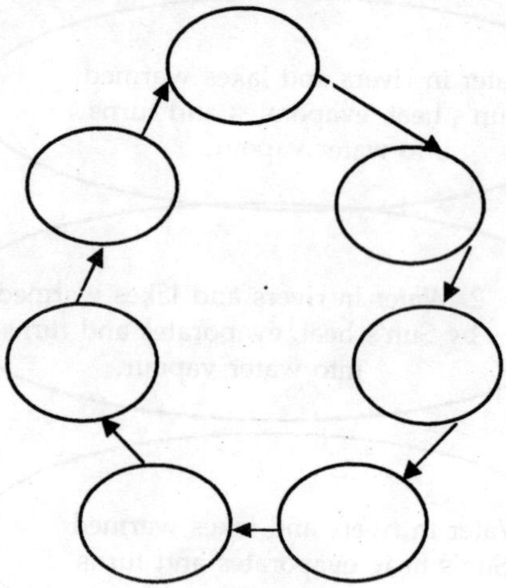

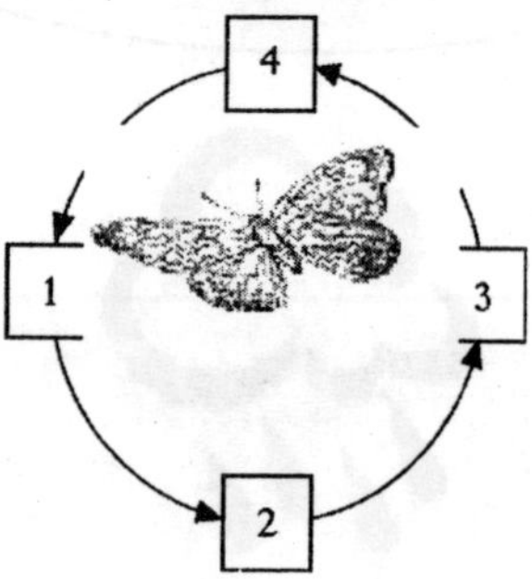

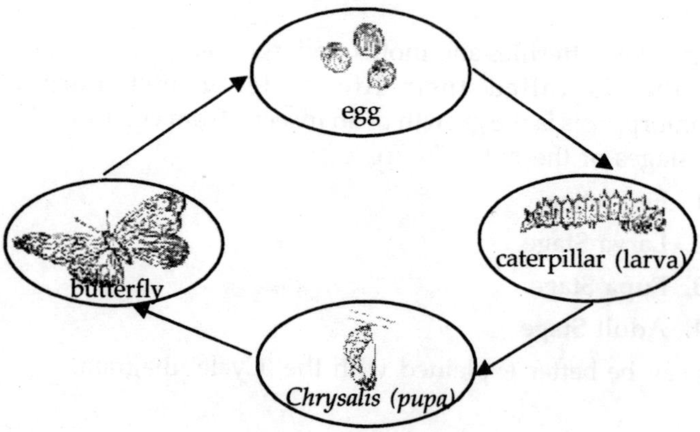

Lifecycle of the Butterfly

A butterfly usually lays 200-500 eggs on plant leaves and stems. Eggs from different butterflies are of different shapes and sizes. The caterpillars hatch from the eggs about five days later.

The caterpillar is also called the larva. Caterpillars first eat their eggshell, then they eat lots of leaves. Each time the caterpillar grows, it needs to shed its old skin or molt. They usually molt five times. After a few weeks the caterpillar stops eating and growing and looks for a place to change.

The caterpillar sheds its skin for the last time and becomes a pupa. The pupa stays inside a hard shell called a chrysalis. Inside the chrysalis, the pupa is changing from a caterpillar's body to a butterfly's body.

The adult butterfly emerges from the chrysalis after several weeks. It looks for another butterfly to mate with. After mating, the female butterfly lays her eggs. The adult butterflies usually live for only two weeks!

Continuum

Continuum is type of graphic organiser that is used to represent a continuum of data that occur in chronological (time) order or in sequential order.

If the topic has a definite beginning and/or ending points, and the data points in between are not discrete, use a continuum.

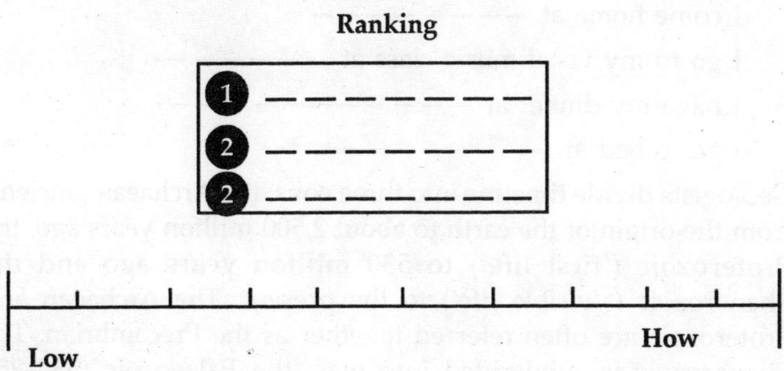

Timeline Diagrams

Timeline diagram is a type of organiser that is used to represent a continuum of data that occur in chronological (time) order or in sequential order. For example a timeline diagram can be used to display milestones in a person's life. In making a timeline, the student must first determine appropriate endpoints for the timeline and important points/dates to label on the continuum.

This type of timeline is used to mark certain years of importance in history or over a particular time period.

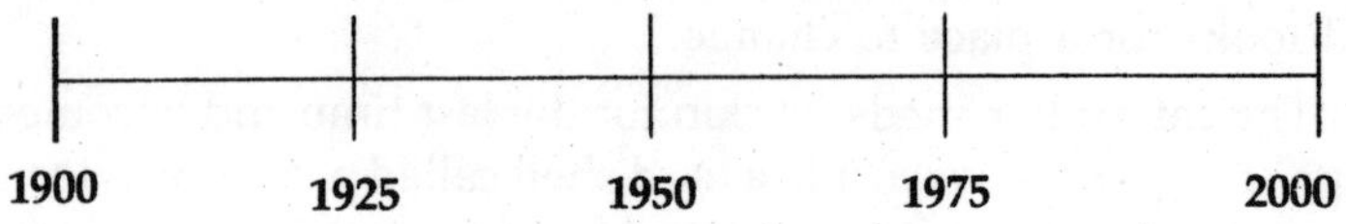

Horizontal Time Line

Learners can be asked to draw timeline, both vertical and horizontal to delineate the different kinds of activities carried out by them at different times of the day.

What I do at different times of the day

I wake up at --------

I go to school at --------

I have my morning recess at ------

I have my lunch break at -------

I have my afternoon recess at -------

I come home at ---------

I go to my vocal music class at --------

I have my dinner at -------------

I go to bed at ----------

Geologists divide timeline into three eons: the Archaean (ancient) from the origin of the earth to about 2,500 million years ago, the Proterozoic ('first life') to 530 million years ago and the Phanerozoic ('visible life') to the present. The Archaean and Proterozoic are often referred together as the Precambrian. The Phanarozoic is subdivided into eras: the Palaeozoic (530–250 million years ago) the Mesozoic (250–65 million years ago) and the Cenozoic (65 million years ago- present). The eras are split into vaious periods. The teritiary and quaternary periods are themselves divided into epochs. These can be illustrated with a vertical timeline like this.

Million Years ago	*Quaternary*	*First Modern humans*
1.8	Tertiary	
65	Cretaceous	Dinosaurs extinct
		First Flowering plants
144	Jurassic	First birds
208	Triassic	First mammals
		First dinosaurs
250	Permian	First archosaurs
286	Carboniferous	First mammal like reptiles
		First reptiles
360	Devonian	First amphibian
		First lobefin fish
		First insects
408	Silurian	First fishes with jaws
438	Ordovician	First land plants
		First jawless fishes
505	Cambrian	
		First shellfish
530	Precambrian	
3500		
4600		Oldest fossils
		Formation of earth

Continuum is used for time lines showing historical events, ages (grade levels in school), degrees of something (weight), shades of meaning, or rating scales (achievement in school).

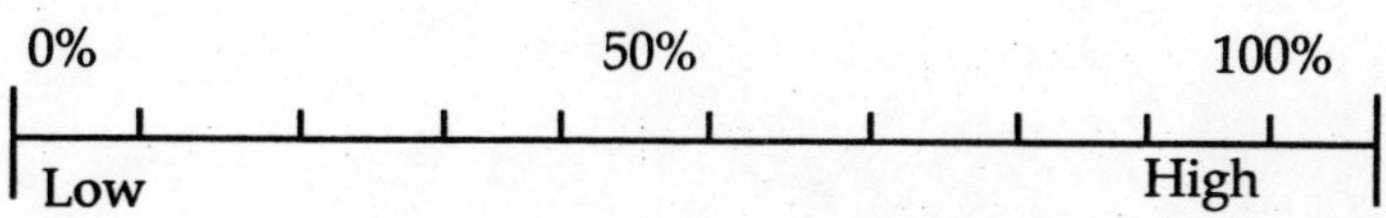

Never Sometimes Often Generally Always
l----------------l----------------l-----------l------------------l

At a lower level, for instance, teaching degrees of comparison to III graders, we can explain with the help of a continuum. For example degrees of comparison for the word, 'good' can be taught as

0%	50%	100%
Good – – – – – –	Better – – – – – –	Best

Thus sequential graphic organisers enable learners to represent information in temporal and chronological order and learn various concepts.

12

Cause and Effect

CHAPTER OVERVIEW

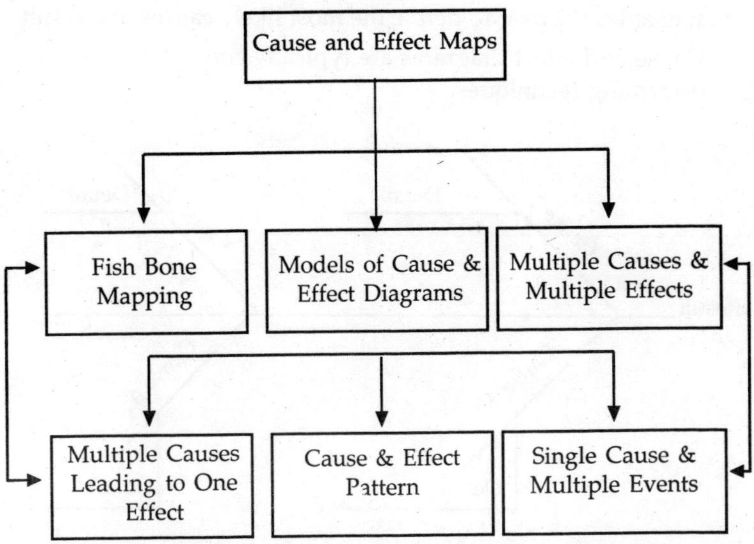

CAUSE AND EFFECT DIAGRAMS ---FISHBONE MAPPING

The technique of cause and effect can be used to illustrate 'why something happened' or 'what will happen'. Analysing the cause can be a complex task. The cause-and-effect diagram is also called the Ishikawa diagram (after its creator, Kaoru Ishikawa of Japan), or the Fishbone Diagram (due to its shape) or Herringbone Map.

A Fishbone Map is used to explore the many aspects or effects of a complex topic, helping the student to organise their thoughts in a simple, visual way. (complex topics - topics that require more details to be enumerated).

The use of colour helps make a fishbone map clearer and easier to interpret.

A Cause and Effect Diagram is an analysis tool to display possible causes of a specific problem or condition.

The process of creating fishbone diagram helps the student to focus on the topic, requires the student to review what they already know in order to organise that knowledge, and helps the students to monitor their growing comprehension of the topic.

It also helps point out the areas where the students must investigate more (where the fishbone is difficult to fill out).

It enables the user to define the most likely causes of a result.

Cause and effect diagrams are typically constructed through brainstorming techniques.

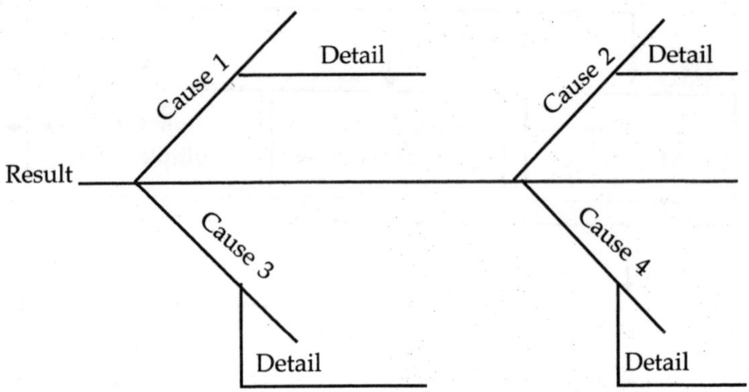

A cause and effect diagram is used for:

1. Identifying potential causes of a problem or issue in an orderly way.
2. Summarising major causes under several categories.

Models of Cause and Effect Diagrams

Disjointed Events - in which each cause has one effect.

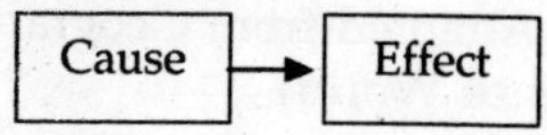

One Cause Leading to Multiple Events - in which one cause has multiple effects.

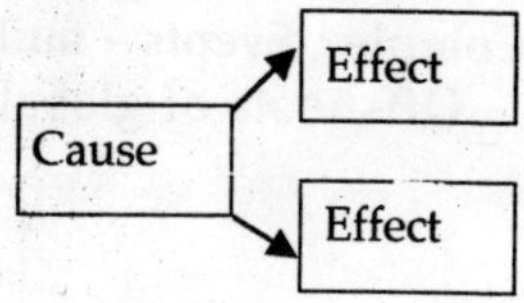

Multiple Causes Leading to One Event - in which multiple causes have one effect (a fishbone diagram can be used for these).

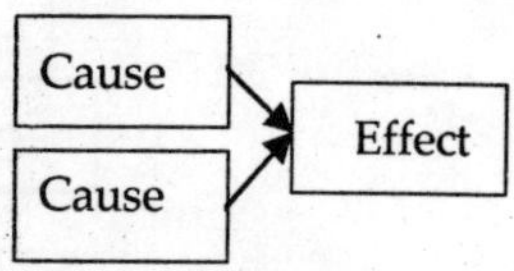

Chain of Events - in which one event initiates another, which causes another, etc., like the domino effect.

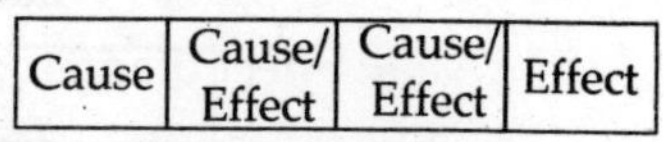

Cycle of Events - in which a cyclic causes/effects are repeated, like a feedback loop.

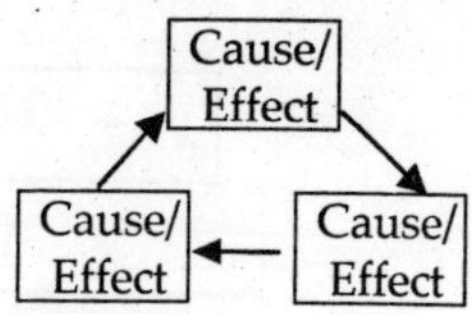

The below diagram beautifully sums up the multiple effects of multiple causes. When there are several causes or reasons for a particular phenomenon, the learner has the problem of arranging them in a significant order of importance. If the reasons follow a logical pattern, the main event is caused by A and A in turn by B and B by C, the organization is predetermined. But sometimes the reasons or causes may be parallel, all contributing to the same result. Then a good strategy is to begin with the least important cause and conclude with the most important.

While developing a topic which is supported by reasons or causes, it has to be borne in mind:

1. Whether the cause is immediate or earlier cause
2. Whether the cause is direct or indirect
3. To consider multiple causes

4. To account for all the links in the sequence of causes

Adapted from Geography by Dougal Dixon, Franklin Watts Science World)

Complex Events - multiple causes & Multiple Effects
Offshoots of globalisation and its repercussions

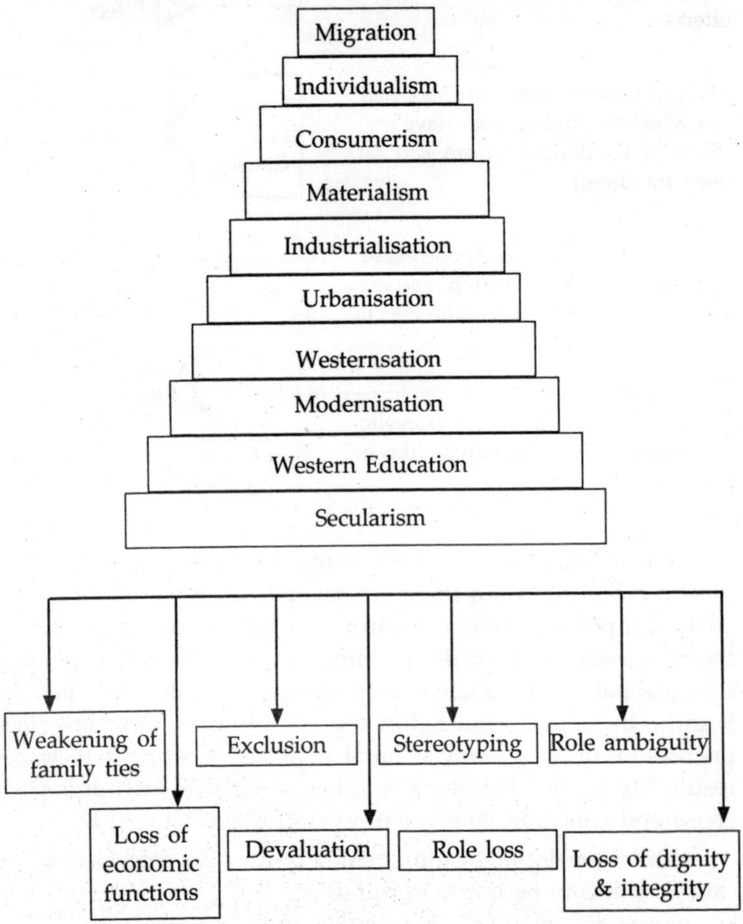

Hills and mountains are slowly worn away over thousands of years by the process of erosion. Erosion takes place everywhere on Earth. There are several forces of erosion: glaciers which carry rocks weighing thousands of tons: frost which causes small cracks on rock sides: strong winds which wear away exposed rocks in deserts. By far the greatest cause of erosion, however, is the action of water on rocks. Water carries chemicals dissolved in it that softens rocks. This softening is the first stage of erosion, called weathering. Rainwater falling on hills runs into streams and rivers and these carry the weathered rock away. Millions of years in the future, your favourite hills will have been worn away completely by erosion.

This is an illustration of multiple causes for one single event which is 'erosion'

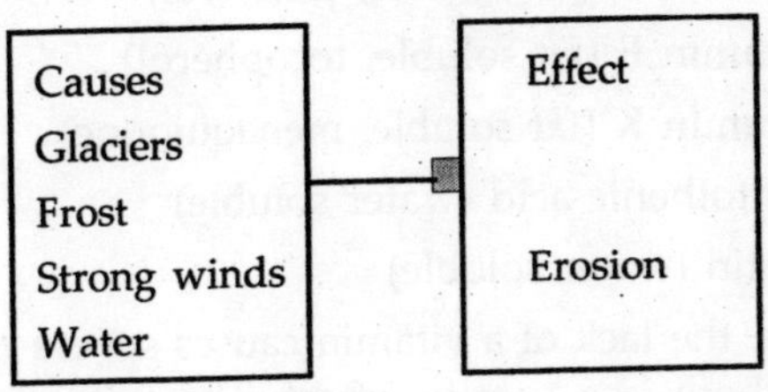

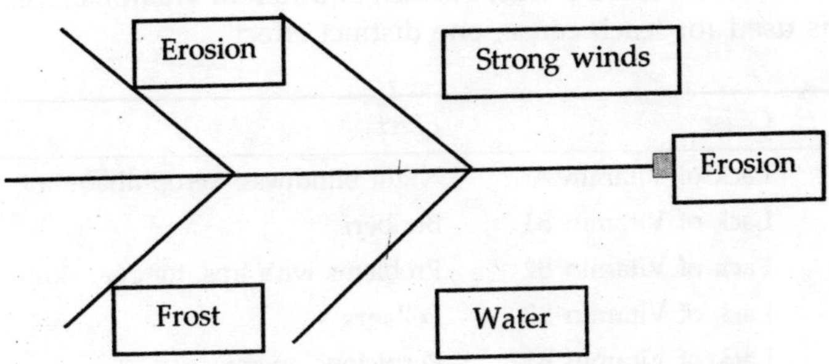

Cause and Effect Pattern

This text structure links reasons with results. It is characterized by an interaction between at least two ideas or events, one taking an action and another resulting from that action.

The human body needs 13 different vitamins:

1. Vitamin A (fat soluble, retinol) comes from beta-carotene in plants; when you eat beta-carotene, an enzyme in the stomach turns it into Vitamin A.

2. Vitamin B (water soluble, several specific vitamins in the complex).
    a) Vitamin B1: Thiamine
    b) Vitamin B2: Riboflavin
    c) Vitamin B3: Niacin
    d) Vitamin B6: Pyridoxine
    e) Vitamin B12: Cyanocobalamin
    f) Folic Acid
3. Vitamin C (water soluble, ascorbic acid)
4. Vitamin D (fat soluble, calciferol)
5. Vitamin E (fat soluble, tocopherol)
6. Vitamin K (fat soluble, menaquinone)
7. Pantothenic acid (water soluble)
8. Biotin (water soluble)

In most cases, the lack of a vitamin causes severe problems. For each cause, there is a specific effect. The following list shows diseases associated with the lack of different vitamins: This chart is used for 'each cause, one distinct effect'.

Cause	*Effect*
Lack of Vitamin A:	Night blindness, xerophthalmia
Lack of Vitamin B1	Beriberi
Lack of Vitamin B2	Problems with lips, tongue, skin,
Lack of Vitamin B3	Pellagra
Lack of Vitamin B12	Pernicious anemia
Lack of Vitamin C	Scurvy
Lack of Vitamin D	Rickets
Lack of Vitamin E	Malabsorption of fats, anemia
Lack of Vitamin K	Poor blood clotting, internal bleeding

A diet of fresh, natural fruits and vegetables provides all the vitamins required for human needs. The content of Vitamin A in some of the fruits and vegetables are given here.

Fruits	*% Vitamin A*
Apricot	45 %
Cantaloupe	100 %
Dried apricots	50 %
Mango	40 %
Watermelon	20 %
Vegetables	*% Vitamin A*
Carrot	270 %
Collards	50 %
Hot chili peppers	80 %
Leaf Lettuce	40 %
Mustard Greens	90 %
Romaine Lettuce	20 %
Spinach	70 %
Sweet Potato	440 %
Tomato	20 %

Single causal factor may result in several effects. Here it is illustrated with the example of 'global warming'. Let us see the different effects of the single cause 'global warming'. Here is an example of 'one cause leading to multiple effects'.

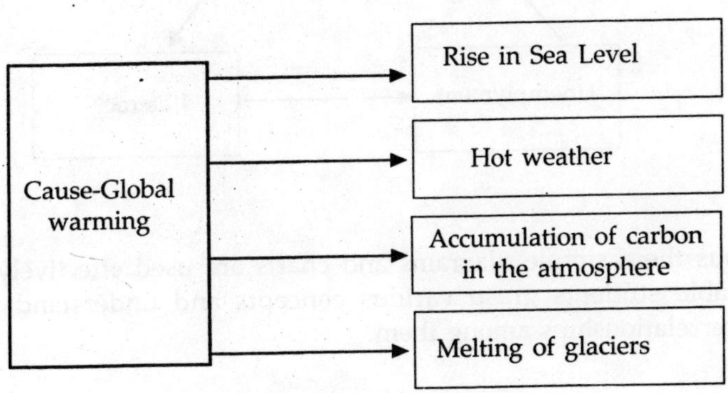

Chain of Events in which one event initiates another, which causes another, etc., like the domino effect. Lack of immunity leads to lack of resistance to diseases and makes a person vulnerable. Once afflicted by a disease, the person feels weak and lethargic.

Physical weakness causes depression and other related mental illness. This can be explained with 'chain of events chart'.

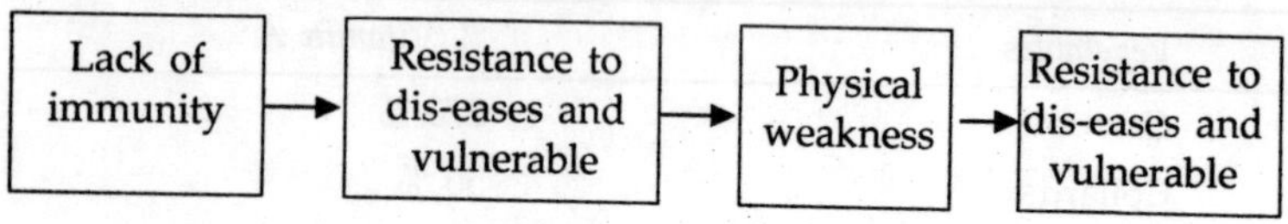

Cycle of Events in which a cyclic causes/effects are repeated, like a feedback loop. The ideal example for cycle of events where causes and effects are repeated is the 'vicious cycle of poverty' – poverty results in illiteracy and this leads to unemployment and this in turn ends in poverty.

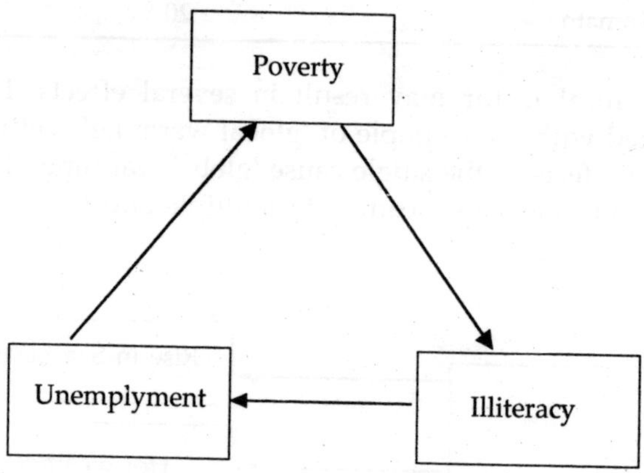

Thus these simple diagrams and charts are used effectively to enable students grasp various concepts and understand the interrelationships among them.

13

Analysing and Brainstorming

Chapter Overview

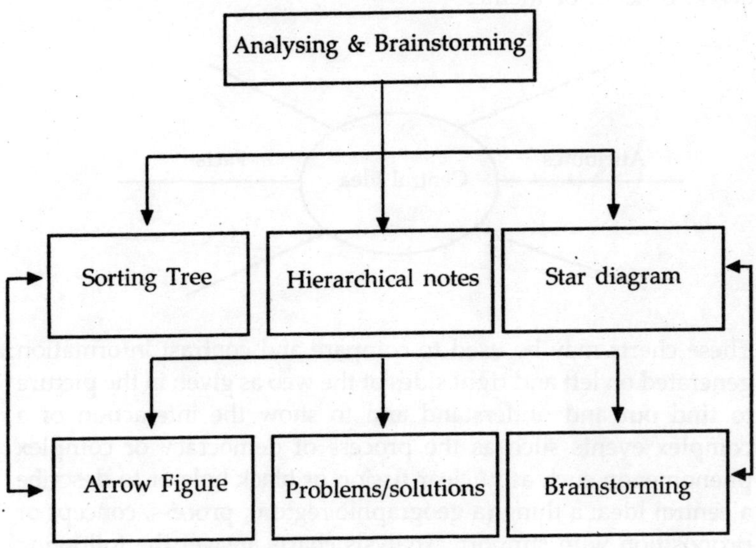

Charts used for Analysis

Understanding current conditions is the starting point of analysis chart. For instance weather reports are analysis charts based on temperature, pressure, wind, moisture and precipitation

The word 'analyse' means to study in detail and examine thoroughly. In its noun form 'analysis', it refers to careful examination of a substance to understand its constituent parts or elements; determine the elements or essential features of (opposed to synthesize): to analyse an argument.

a) to examine critically, so as to bring out the essential elements or give the essence of: to analyse a poem.

a) to examine carefully and in detail so as to identify causes, key factors, possible results, etc. (Webster's. p 74).

b) to break down, break up, dissect; differentiate, make a distinction, sharpen or refine a distinction; subdivide; catalog, list, file; assay, titrate; reduce to elements, resolve (Chapman, 1977).

Analysing attributes are used in general to give details about facts, definitions, attributes and examples related to a single topic, event, concept or theme.

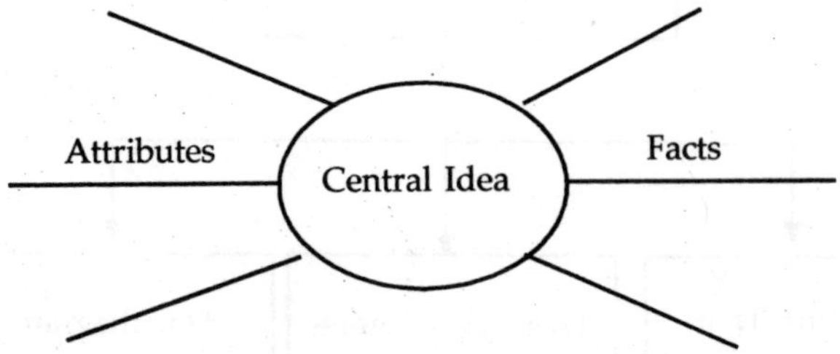

These charts may be used to compare and contrast information generated on left and right sides of the web as given in the picture to find out and understand and to show the interaction of a complex events such as the process of democracy or complex phenomenon such as nuclear fission or black hole or to describe a central idea: a thing (a geographic region), process, concept or proposition with support. Analysis charts answer the following questions:

- What is the central idea?
- What are its attributes?
- What are its functions?
- What are the factors that cause X?
- How do they interrelate?
- Are the factors that cause X the same as those that cause X to persist?

Tree Diagrams

Tree Diagrams are a type of graphic organiser that shows how items are related to one another. The tree's trunk represents the main topic, and the branches represent relevant facts, factors, influences, traits, people, or outcomes. The diagram starts at a single node, with branches emanating to additional nodes just like the branches of a tree. In this type of diagram, the analysis will begin at the first blank node. A decision or event will then lead to node A or B. From these secondary nodes, additional decisions or events will occur leading to the third level of nodes, until a final conclusion is reached.

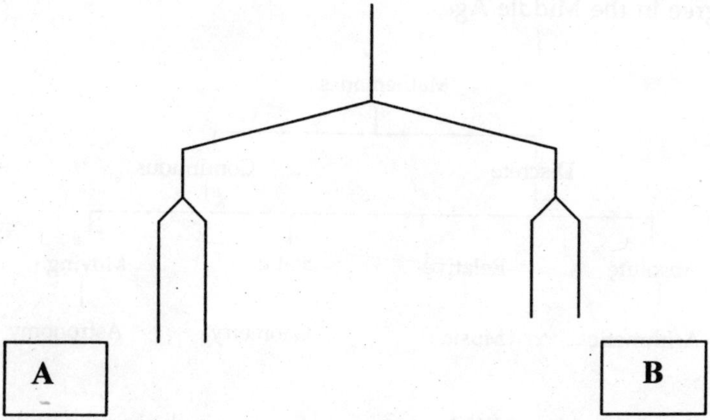

Tree diagrams can be used to sort items or classify them. A family tree is an example of a tree diagram. Other examples of trees are cladistic trees (used in biological classification) and dichotomous trees (used to detemine what group a specimen belongs to in biology). Tree diagrams are also used as visuals in statistics to document the outcomes of probabalistic events (like tossing a coin).

Structured Overview

Structured overview technique uses key vocabulary to highlight the main concepts of a topic to drive home the interrelationships among them. A structured overview that previews and highlights important information and the interrelationships of ideas is a very useful graphic organiser as it helps the learners to have a bird's eye view of the topic – learners have the complete picture or the whole picture of the topic as in the following example.

The quadrivium

While speaking of groups of four, we owe to the Pythagoreans, the division of mathematics into four groups, giving the famous *Quadrivium of knowledge,* the four subjects needed for a bachelor's degree in the Middle Ages.

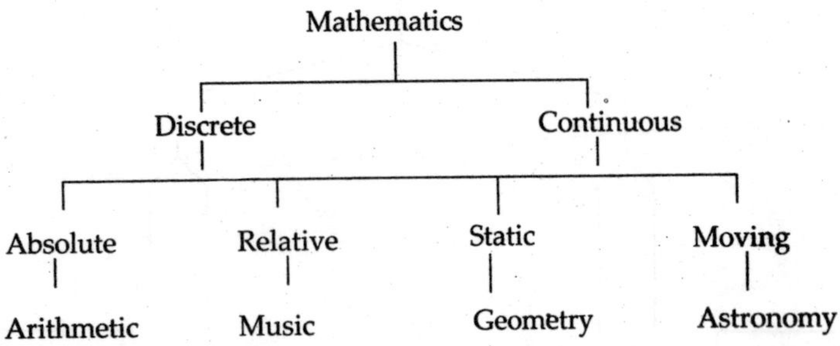

While teaching how different groups of organs in the human body work together as systems – Each system has a vital role to play and different organs that comprise each system , 'Structured Overview' is the ideal tool.

Hierarchical Notes

A hierarchy is also like a flowchart, except each subordinate step may have more than one branch. A useful, familiar tool for organising ideas into a hierarchy is the Pyramid diagram. Maslow's hierarchy of human needs and Kohlberg's moral stages come to mind as examples that conform to this format. The tool is, in short, a means of organising information or ideas into a hierarchy.

Another popular hierarchical map used in education is 'Edgar Dale's Cone of Experiences'. In the cone, the most concrete experiences are placed at the bottom of the cone and the most abstract experiences at the top. At the bottom of the cone, the direct purposeful experiences are represented. At the pinnacle of the cone the verbal symbols are represented. In the scale of the directness, the verbal symbols are the least. So we come to know that as we move upward from the base of the cone, the level of directness decreases. Thus "demonstrations" are less direct than the "dramatised experiences". The verbal symbols represented at the top of the cone are extremely abstract in nature. While teaching, we should try to give all these experiences to the learners. If we can use more aids from the bottom of the cone, the more concrete and understandable will be our teaching and so more effective will be the learning process.

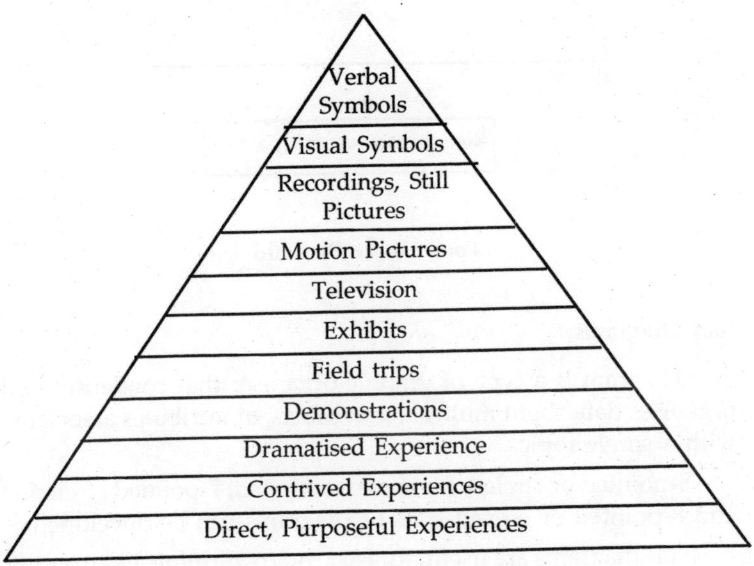

Food guide Pyramid

This pyramid serves as a guide to daily food choices. The breadth of the base indicates the foods that contribute complex carbohydrates and fibre with riboflavin, thiamine, niacin, iron, protein, magnesium and other nutrients that have to be given utmost emphasis and have to be consumed the most. The tip is the smallest, that is, foods that contain fats, sugar, alcohol, oils etc., have to be used very sparingly as they provide few nutrients.

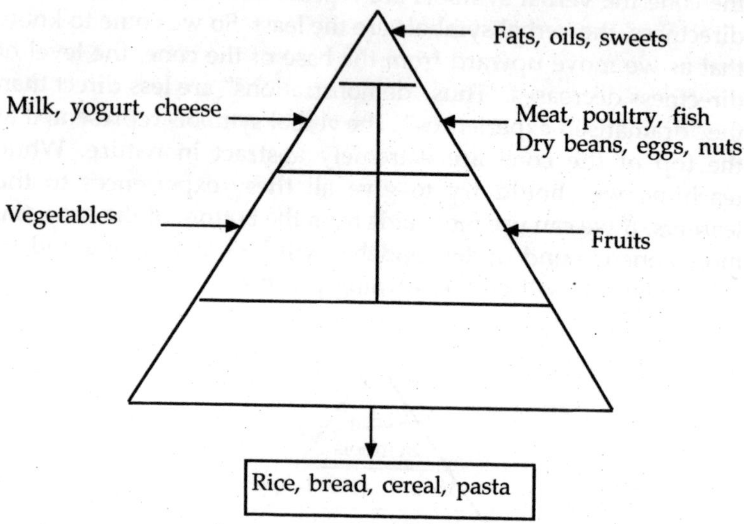

Food Guide Pyramid

Star Diagrams

Star Diagram is a type of graphic organiser that condenses and organises data about multiple traits, facts, or attributes associated with a single topic.

5-pointed or circled, 6-pointed or circled, 7-pointed or circled and 8-pointed or circled stars or diagrams can be developed.

Star diagrams are useful for basic brainstorming about a topic or simply listing all the major traits related to a theme.

Portraying the five kingdoms of living things in a Pentagram which is popularly known as Star of David is rather interesting.

The five kingdoms of living things are:

Monerans
Protists
Fungi
Plants
Animals

For example, a star diagram can be used to create a graphic display describing all you know about the five major divisions or kingdoms of living things - when they lived, what kinds there were, how big they were, what they ate, where fossils have been found, etc. or a graphic display of methods that help your study skills (like taking notes, reading, doing homework, memorizing, etc.).

Arrow Figure

This kind of figure helps to understand various features, characteristics, aspects, perspectives of a problem, object, event, concept etc., For instance, this diagram can be used to teach simple concepts such as different **'directions'** to pupils in any lower grade - the 'Eight big arrows' pointing to 'North, East, South and West, Northeast, Northwest, Southeast and Southwest'. This can also be used to indicate the eight dimensions or features of an object or phenomenon.

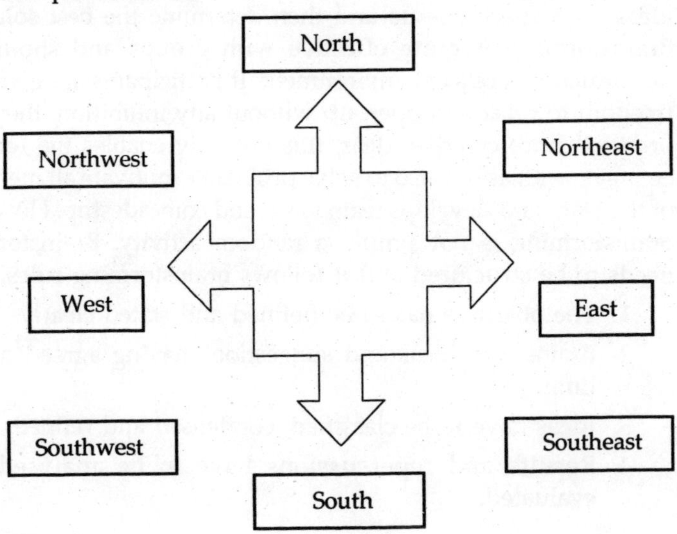

Problem/Solution

Problem/Solution requires students to identify a problem and consider multiple solutions and possible results.

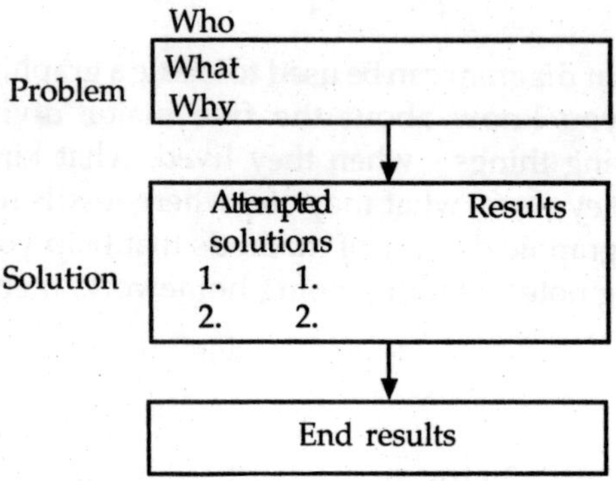

Brainstorming

Brainstorming is a group creativity technique designed to generate a large number of ideas for the solution of a problem. Brainstorming can be a powerful technique to generate lots of ideas on a specific issue and then determine the best solution. Brainstorming is quite effective with groups and should be performed in a relaxed environment. If participants are given the freedom to relax and open up without any inhibition, they will produce more creative ideas; this not only enables the team to create new ideas but also to solve problems, motivate all members of the team and develops team spirit and comradeship. However, brainstorming is not simply a random activity. Brainstorming needs to be structured and it follows brainstorming rules.

1. The objective has to be defined and stated clearly.
2. Brainstorm ideas and suggestions having agreed a time limit.
3. Ideas have to be classified, condensed and refined.
4. Results and repercussions have to be analysed and evaluated.

5. Decisions have to be prioritised.
6. Proper monitoring and follow- up are essential.

Viewing and analysing things from different angles and perspectives help to see them clearly and completely. Conventional verbal brainstorming often does not produce the best ideas. Visual brainstorming, using images and objects and actions to build ideas on the other hand can be highly effective. In other words, visual brainstorming is about collaboratively generating ideas by using visuals and objects such as coloured construction paper, tape, string, card, pens etc., without using the spoken or written word.

Visual Brainstorming Rules

a) Collecting ideas from participants without being critical or judgemental is the first step.
b) All ideas are collected; nothing is considered trivial or silly.
c) When the brainstorming session is in operation, no discussion is carried out.
d) All participants are encouraged to build up on others' ideas.
e) Setting time limit for the brainstorming will help all participants to be committed and focused.

Synectics

Synectics is a creative problem solving approach that stimulates the thought process and helps an individual to look at a seemingly unrelated phenomenon and establish relevant connections. This method was developed by George M. Prince and William J. J. Gordon in 1960 . The most important tool in this approach is metaphor or analogy. The approach, which is often used by groups, can help students develop creative responses to problem solving, to retain new information, to assist in generating writing, and to explore social and disciplinary problems. "It helps users break existing mind sets and internalise abstract concepts. Synectics can be used with all ages and works well with those who withdraw from traditional methods". (Couch, 1993)

"Creativity is nothing more than following a systematic process, allowing random connections to take place, and using your intuition to develop unique solutions. Oh, by the way, it's much easier and much more fun when you work with others throughout the process." – Doug

As an invention tool, Synectics invented a technique called "springboarding" for getting creative beginning ideas. For the development of beginning ideas, the method incorporates brainstorming and deepens and widens it with metaphor; it also adds an important evaluation process for Idea Development, which takes embryonic new ideas that are attractive but not yet feasible and builds them into new courses of action which have the commitment of the people who will implement them.

In order to understand a concept or a problem completely, the concept or the problem has to be defined. It has to be analysed by comparing and contrasting with other concepts and problems. In classroom situations, the learners have to be led by a process that enables them to gain three dimensional view of the concept or the problem.

Concept Definition	*Similarities*	*Differences*	*Comparison*	*Perceptions of the learners*	*Solution*

In case the learners have to know about people, similar charts can be used by focusing on the physical features, skills, interests, attitudes, psychological characteristics etc.

14

Chart Diagrams / Matrices

Chapter Overview

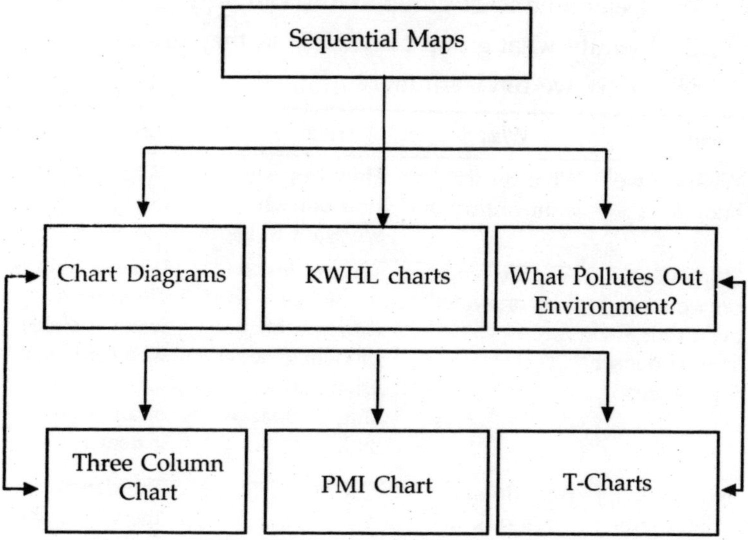

Chart Diagrams

Chart Diagram also called matrix diagram or table is a type of graphic organiser that condenses and organises data about multiple traits associated with many items or topics. Charts can be used to show attributes of items, to compare and contrast topics, and to evaluate information.

Charts can be used:

a) to create a display of characteristics
b) to show attributes of items
c) to compare and contrast topics
d) to show key inventions
e) to evaluate information.

KWHL Charts or Matrix

This type of chart is used for predicting and evaluating by activating learners' prior knowledge. It is a group instruction activity that serves as a model for active thinking during reading.

K - Recall what group KNOWs about the subject.
W - Determine what group WANTs to learn.
L - Identify what group LEARNED as they read.
H - HOW we can learn more

Know	*What*	*How*	*Learn*
What do we know?	What do we want to find out?	How can we find out what we want to learn?	What did we learn?
Ships float on water even though steel is denser than water.	Why do ships float on water?	We can test a variety of different boat models to see what causes a ship to float or sink.	When a ship is filled with water it sinks, when it has a large amount of air in it, it floats.
Ships sink when there is a hole in the hull. The Titanic is related to for example.	Why do some ships sink in water?		The density of the whole ship both the ship itself and the air within.

Animals belong to two broad groups – vertebrates and invertebrates. Invertebrates are animals that do not have backbones. Insects belong to a large group of invertebrates known as arthropods. Other members of this group include centipedes, spiders and scorpions and crabs and shrimps. All insects have six legs and a body divided into three sections: the head, thorax and abdomen. Insects have a pair of antennae on their heads which they use to smell, touch and to pick up vibrations. Most insects have one or two pairs of wings.

While explaining this, matrix can be used.

Types of invertebrates	*No. of legs*	*No. of Body segments*	*No of antennae*	*wings*	*Example*
Insects	6	3	2	2	Butterfly
Arachnid	8	2	0	0	Spider, scorpion
Myriapods	200	Multiple	2	0	Millipedes
Crustacea	10	2	4	0	Crab

The graphic organiser that is used here helps to demonstrate perhaps the widest range of complexity - is the matrix. Matrices are constructs of rows and columns. They can span a range from simple, one column 1 x n matrices to unlimited n x n matrices. They can be used to compare and contrast two items, or they can be used to list objects cross-referenced with the attributes of each object. Charts are used to compare characteristics among a group of items.

While teaching nouns that change when given in plural form and nouns that remain the same, two columns and any number of rows can be made use of. For example

Nouns that stay the same

Singular	*Plural*
Deer	Deer
Sheep	Sheep
Cattle	Cattle
Trout	Trout
Fish	Fish
Crowd	Crowd

Nouns that change

Singular	*Plural*
Child	Children
Goat	Goats
man	Men
Boy	Boys
Ox	Oxen
Foot	Feet

Here is a three-column chart that is illustrated with an example.

What Pollutes Our Environment?

While Raju and I were returning from our school, we saw buses, lorries and huge trucks emitting black carbon monoxide fumes. The fumes made everything around look nasty, dirty, black and grimy. We also saw dogs, pigs and cats and even some children making in the streets. There was a neat toilet but the children were not using the toilets. They preferred to make it on the pavements. Raju wasn't looking where he was walking and he stepped on this dirt. His shoes smelled terrible and we found a tap on the roadside and we washed his shoes there.

Across the street from the public toilet, nasty and filthy stench was coming and it was really overwhelming. Next to the toilet, we saw a factory. The smokestacks had black clouds of dirt pouring out of them. One factory smelled like soiled cabbage and bad eggs. Raju said it was probably the smell of sulfur. There was also a lot of uncollected garbage spilling into the street in front of one of the factories. We also saw people drop papers, plastic bags, banana peels and garbage in the street as they walked by us. We saw a butcher throwing away a huge pile of animal waste onto the street.

Three Column Chart to explain different types of pollutants and how they affect the sensory organs.

Pollutants that Affect My Senses

Eyes	*Ears*	*Nose*
Garbage piles	Loud radios	Garbage
Graffiti, advertising signs/ hoardings/posters	Sound from Car/ truck/ bus horns	Animal waste
Street clutter	Truck engines	Chemical waste
Butcheries on the roadside	Drilling/ construction	Effluent and stagnant water
Smog	Welding and sawing noise from foundries, lathes and timber shops and factories	Burning of tyres, rubber and plastics on the roadside
Smoke	Tavern brawls, quarrels and fights	Putrefied vegetables, fruits etc.,
Run down buildings	Fireworks, crackers etc.,	Ditch and sewage blocks due to improper drainage.
Effluent water	Amplifiers and speakers –public meetings religious festivals, celebrations etc.,	Roadside urination and improper sanitary conditions.
Sparks from fireworks, welding etc.,	Markets, overcrowded places	Smoke from factories and distilleries etc.,
Spitting, excretion etc.,	Noise made by machines in factories	Smoke from fireworks, crackers etc.,
Overcrowded places	Sirens	Fish stalls, trucks loaded with fish, chicken, poultries etc.,
Dead animals	People talking loudly	Unremoved dead animals left on the roadside.
Road blocks		Black-topping of the roads- smell of bitumen, tar etc

PMI Chart

PMI Charts are a type of a three-column graphic organiser in which the student examines the merits, demerits and implications associated with a topic, a decision, or an idea. For example, a student can use a PMI chart to help organise his / her thoughts about making a decision such as getting a pet. In management parlance, this kind of analysis is known as SWAT analysis. S stands for 'strengths', W for 'weaknesses', A for 'Advantages' and T for 'threats'.

Construction of a House or Owning a home

PlusesMinuses	*Interesting Features*	
Tax deduction	Cost & affordability	Decorations
Proud owner	Paying property tax	Landscaping
Amenities & choices	Repairs & Maintenance	House Owners Society

T-Charts

T – Charts are a type of chart, a graphic organiser in which a student lists and examines two facets of a topic, like the pros and cons associated with it, its advantages and disadvantages, facts versus opinions, myths versus realities etc. For example, a student can use a T-chart to help graphically organise thoughts about getting a dog as a pet.

Pros	*Cons*
Guards the house	Taking care of the dog
Compassion for animals	Cost of food
Companion / friend	Veterinary visits

Evaluating the pros and cons of a topic (for example, adopting a new invention), enumerating the problems and solutions associated with an action (for example, analysing the plot of a book or a topic like poor nutrition), listing facts versus opinions of a theme after reading fiction or a newspaper article come under T-charts.

Uses of T-Charts

a) For example, a student can use a T-chart to help graphically organize thoughts about:

b) Making a decision by comparing resulting advantages and disadvantages (like getting a pet or taking a new job),

c) Evaluating the pros and cons of a topic (for example, adopting a new invention),

d) Enumerating the problems and solutions associated with an action (for example, analysing the plot of a book or a topic like poor nutrition),

e) Listing facts vs. opinions of a theme (great to use after reading a selection of text or a news article),

f) Explaining the strengths and weaknesses of a piece of writing (useful after reading a piece of persuasive or expository writing),

g) Listing any two characteristics of a topic (like the main ideas for a given topic and a salient detail for each idea).

Simple diagrams, charts and matrices direct the pupils' understanding of the text as these are based on individual responses.

15

Miscellaneous Graphic Organisers

Chapter Overview

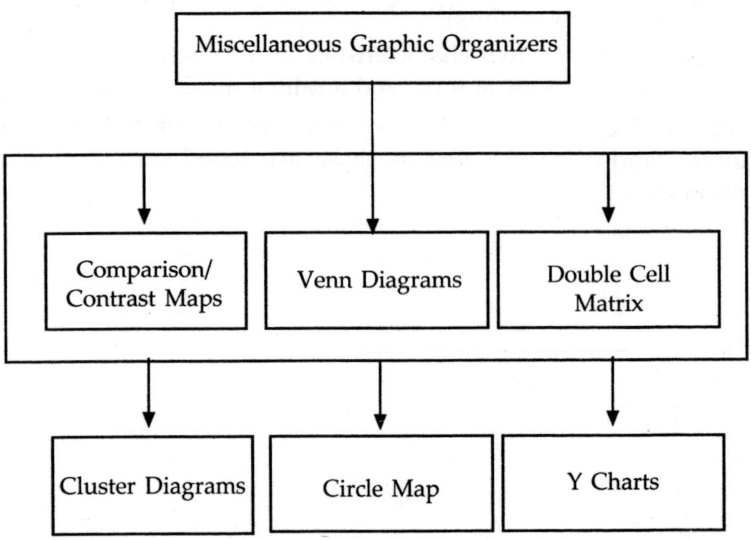

Comparison/Contrast Patterns

Comparing and contrasting patterns are used to analyse similarities and differences between two things such as people, places, events, ideas, topics etc. by placing differing or similar characteristics in either on the left or right sections of the column.

Key Frame Questions

— What are being compared?

— How are they similar?

— How are they different?

VENN DIAGRAMS

The English mathematician John Venn invented the Venn diagram in 1880. In mathematics, Venn diagrams are used to visualise the relationship between two or three sets. Venn diagrams, familiar constructs for portraying set theory in mathematics, can be applied to other disciplines as well. They can be used in the same way as in mathematics - for demonstrating the ways in which two or more sets of data coincide. They effectively depict the similarities and differences between groups. Venn diagrams can be used for making comparisons and contrasts between people, things, events, books, animals, characters in novels etc., They consist of two or more intersecting circles (two or three overlapping circles) that depict relationships among concepts. They are especially useful for use with younger children. String or colored yarn can be used to make circles on the floor. Physical objects and pictures are often used.

Venn diagram showing the similarities and differences between acids and alkalines can be made. Venn diagrams answer the following questions.

— What items do you want to compare or contrast?

— How are the items the same (intersecting portion)?

— How are the items different (non intersecting portion)?

Figure below represents a simple, two group Venn diagram.

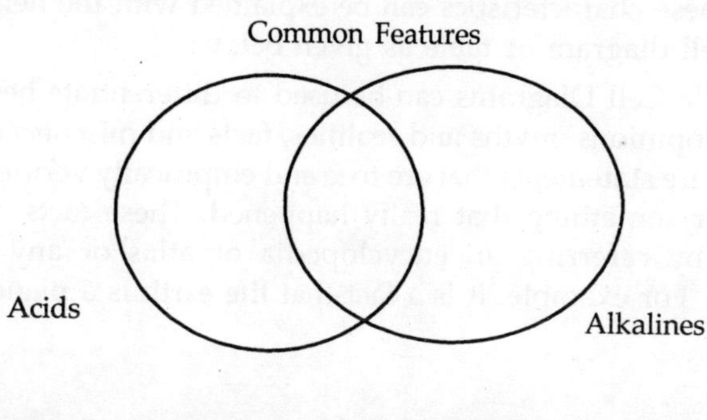

Compare the characteristics of plant and animal cells using this Venn diagram and certain common characteristics. Pick two animals, then compare and contrast them using a Venn diagram. Label the Venn diagram of the similarities and differences between butterflies and moths. Make a Venn diagram showing the similarities and differences between frogs and toads. On this printout, the student classifies geometric figures by shape, size, and shading by placing them in Venn diagrams

A Double Cell Diagram is an excellent substitute for a Venn Diagram for comparing likenesses and differences. Good for use with younger children. Use cells and links with younger children to help them create more complex webs and maps in the future. String, hula hoops, colored yarn, colored paper, colored pens all can be useful to make cells on the floor or wall for younger children. A good tool to launch writing about what is similar and what is not. Here is an example of comparison chart.

Key Characteristics of Elementary and Middle School Learners

Pre school students (ages 2-4) absorb language effortlessly and imitate speech sounds well; are self-centred and do not work well in groups; respond best to activities relating to their own interests; have as short attention span; respond best to concrete experiences.

Primary students (ages 5-7 KG, I & II Graders) learn best through concrete experiences, are imaginative and respond well to stories of fantasy and dramatic play; learn through oral language and can develop good oral skills, pronunciation and intonation when they have a good model; have a short attention span and require large muscle activity; need structured and specific directions and regular routines.

All these characteristics can be explained with the help of a double cell diagram or table as given below:

Double Cell Diagrams can be used to differentiate between facts and opinions, myths and realities, facts and misconceptions etc. Facts are statements that are true and empirically verified and proved or something that really happened. These facts can be checked by referring an encyclopedia or atlas or any other reference. For example, it is a fact that the earth is a planet and it is round. Opinions express how a person feels about something – opinions do not have to be based upon logical reasoning. For example, it is an opinion that all Indians are good in mathematics. A student can use one of these graphic organizers to help determine which parts of a news article, debate, or essay are facts and which are opinions. This is a useful tool for developing critical thinking skills.

Double Cell Diagram

Elementay School Learners	*Middle School Learners*
These learners learn language effortlessly	Primary students learn best through concrete experiences
Elementary School learners imitate speech sounds well	These children are imaginative
These children are self-centred	These children are fond of fantasies and dramatic play
They do not work well in groups.	At this age, they develop good oral skills
They like to take part in activities that are of interest to them	They like muscular activities and physical plays
They have short attention span	These children also have short attention span
These children respond very well to concrete experiences	They need structured specific direction.

While teaching how different groups of organs in the human body work together as systems – Each system has a vital role to play and different organs that comprise each system , 'Structured Overview' is the ideal tool.

Cluster/Cloud Diagrams

Cluster diagram (also called cloud diagrams) is a type of non-linear graphic organiser that can help to generate ideas, images and feelings based upon a central topic or a stimulus word. Using this type of diagram, the student can more easily brainstorm a theme, associate about an idea, or explore a new subject. As students cluster, their thoughts tumble out, enlarging their word bank for writing and often enabling them to see patterns in their ideas. Clustering may be a class or an individual activity.

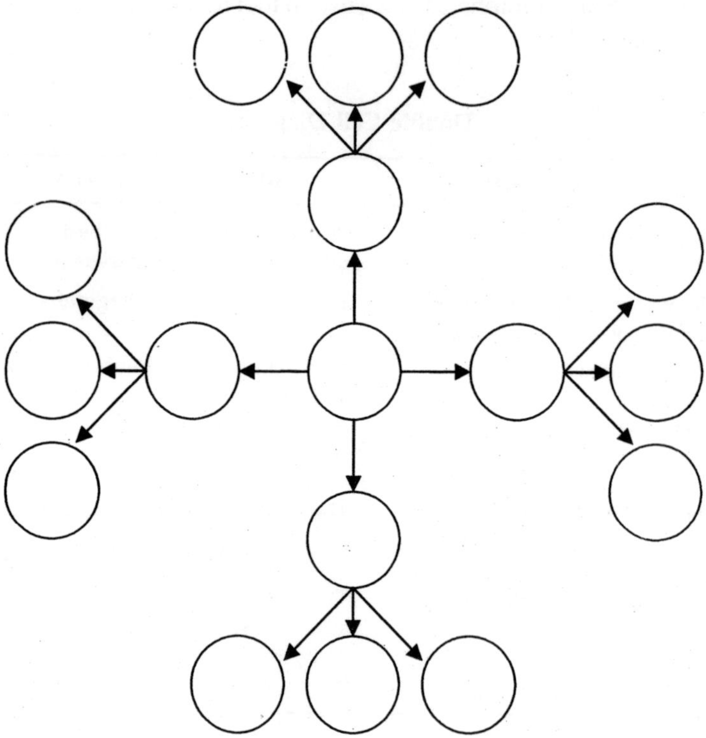

Cluster diagrams enable learners to develop the following comprehension skills:

a) recall directly stated facts
b) recognise and formulate main ideas
c) select facts to support main idea
d) extrapolate/interpret
e) appreciate what is read
f) determine authors intent

g) recognise schema
h) define and use vocabulary
i) recognise relationships
j) create or invent
k) solve problems
l) make decisions

To create a cluster diagram, the student first thinks of as many terms or ideas relating to the stimulus topic as possible (and then writes the second-level ideas in circles attached to the main topic) - this first step is drawing a circle or creating a star diagram. Then the student explores each of these new second-level ideas in turn, and for each, finds as many related ideas as possible (and adds these third-level terms to the diagram around the idea). If more detail is desired, the previous step can be repeated for each of the third-level ideas (or more).

For example, a cluster diagram can be used to create a graphic display or to brainstorm a topic such as pollution. The first level of ideas could be specific types of pollution (like air pollution, water pollution, polluted soil, etc.), and the second-level could be details on each of those subtopics (for air pollution, you could include causes of air pollution, effects of air pollution, how to stop it, etc.). You could go on to include further details on these third-level topics, and more levels, until you are out of ideas. Color coding can be very helpful in making an easy-to-understand cluster diagram.

Circle Map

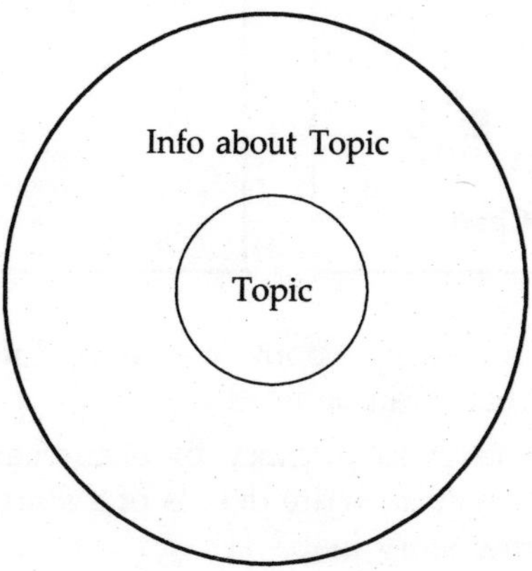

Circle maps are almost similar to cluster maps; but, here only two or three layers of information are used to enhance the comprehension skills of the learners.

Y-Chart or Pie Charts

Y-Charts are a type of a three-part graphic organiser that helps the student organise what they know with respect to three qualities or for displaying information about the percentages or parts of a whole.

For example, a student can describe what they know about a plant – its botanical name, where is it found and what are its uses or a character in a novel – his / her physical stature and appearance according to the author, his / her role in the novel or play, how he /she achieves the objectives.

An object can be delineated in detail pointing out its three factors such as

— What is it made of?

— What does it look like?

— What are its uses?

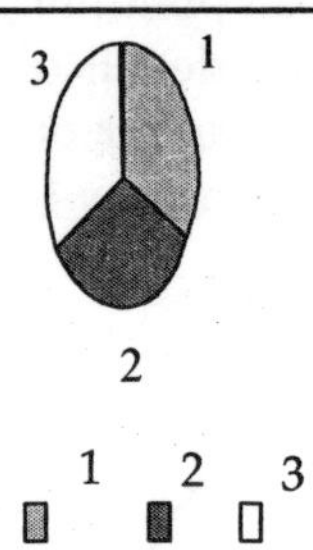

Y--Chart

1. botanical name
2. where is it found
3. what are its uses

While critically reviewing a book or a novel, 'Literature Analysis Map' as given below can be used.

At a lower level in primary or elementary school level, children can be asked to write details of a story they have read as in the following story map.

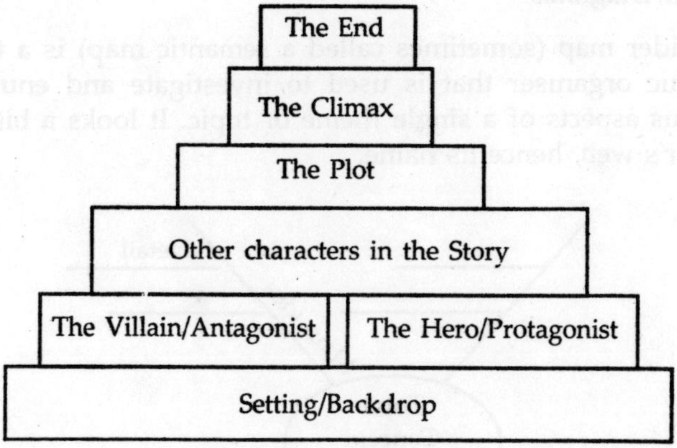

Literature Analysis Map

Story Map

Operating Systems

The interaction between the hardware and software is managed by a set of programmes known as 'operating system' of a computer; it monitors all the operations of the computer as illustrated in the figure given below.

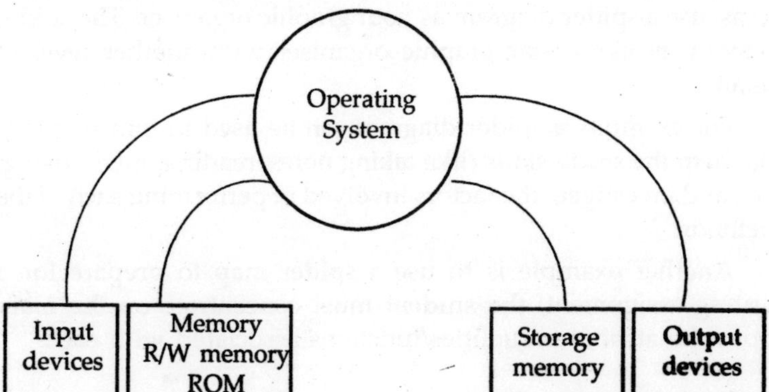

Spider Diagrams

A Spider map (sometimes called a semantic map) is a type of graphic organiser that is used to investigate and enumerate various aspects of a single theme or topic. It looks a bit like a spider's web, hence its name.

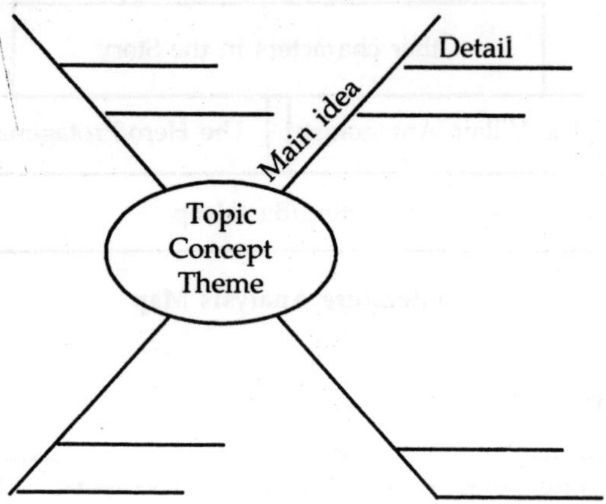

The process of creating a spider diagram helps the student focus on the topic, requires the student to review what he already knows in order to organise that knowledge, and helps the student to monitor his growing comprehension of the topic. It also helps point out the areas where the student must investigate more. If the topic at hand involves investigating attributes associated with a single topic, and then obtaining more details on each of these ideas, use a spider diagram as your graphic organiser. The spider diagram is like a star graphic organiser with another level of detail.

For example, a spider diagram can be used to find methods that help the study skills (like taking notes, reading, memorising, etc.) and investigate the factors involved in performing each of the methods.

Another example is to use a spider map to prepare for a writing assignment; the student must concentrate on the main topic, the attributes/qualities/functions associated with each.

Key frame questions:

- What is the central idea?
- What are its attributes?
- What are its functions?

Suppose the lesson is on "River', a semantic map that can be created to link various concepts associated with river will look like this.

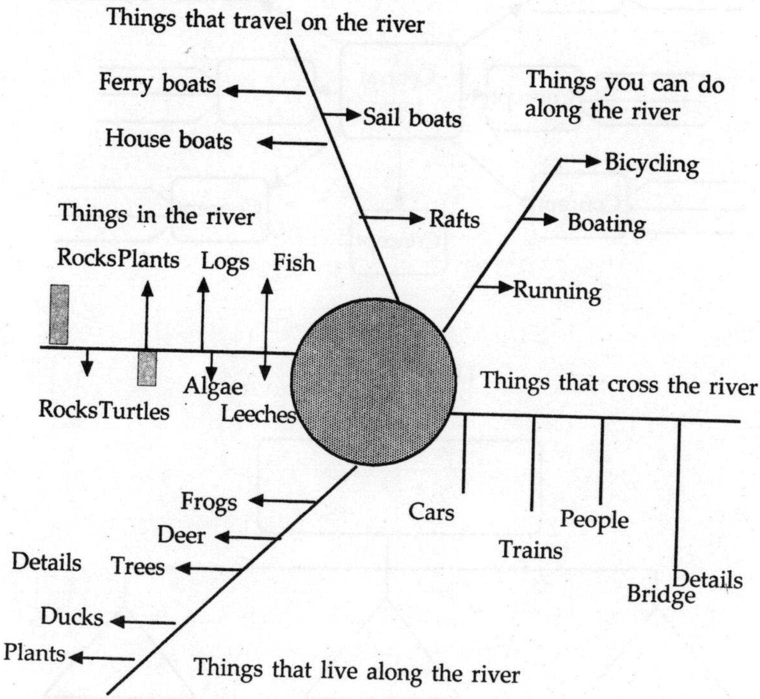

Comprehension Skills

a) recall directly stated facts
b) recognise and formulate main ideas
c) select facts to support main idea
d) extrapolate/interpret
e) recognise schema

f) recognise relationships

g) solve problems

h) make decisions

Descriptive Pattern

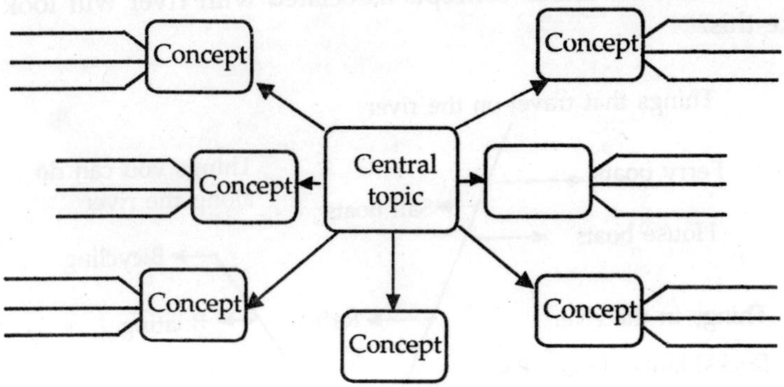

Listing Pattern

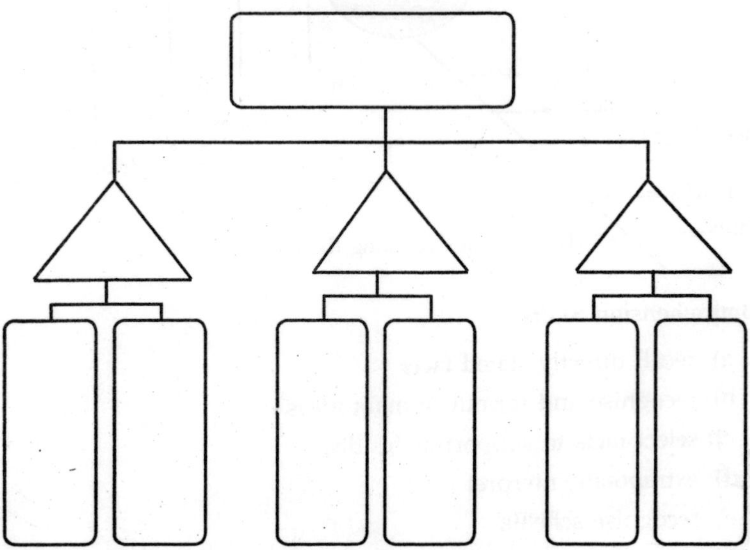

Spider maps are well suited for depicting a central concept surrounded by related information. This may consist of an object and its attributes, or a primary concept with arms and legs for each major supporting idea. A branch from each leg for details of each idea may be included. Another example consists of a central proposition with supporting material, quotes, data, and examples, each on their own leg.

Descriptive Pattern. This text structure gives more information about a topic by attributes, examples, or elaboration.

Graphic organisers can be used to help formulate and organise a scientific experiment. A scientific experiment involves many steps such as observation, gathering evidence, formulating a hypothesis, designing an experiment, conducting an experiment, analysing and summarising results and drawing conclusions.

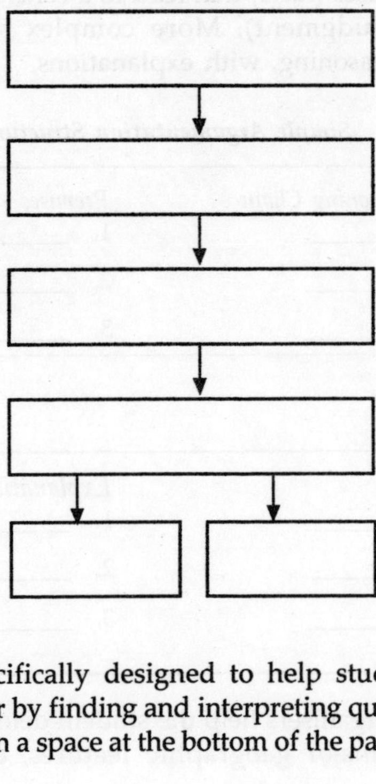

Inference Notes

This tool is specifically designed to help students analyse a fictional character by finding and interpreting quotes by or about the character; then a space at the bottom of the page asks students to make inferences about the character, incorporating examples from the graphic organizer.

Premises

1. ____________________
2. ____________________
3. ____________________

Conclusion

Argumentation structures can range from simple to complex. They represent the logical evaluation of an argument, presenting support for drawing a particular conclusion. Simple structures represent premises (facts) that lead to a conclusion (a deduction, inference, or judgment). More complex structures contain sequences of reasoning, with explanations.

Simple Argumentation Structure

Premises - Reasoning Chain	*Premises - Reasoning Chain*
1. ____________	1. ____________
2. ____________	2. ____________
3. ____________	3. ____________

Conclusion

Explanations	*Explanations*
1. ____________	1. ____________
2. ____________	2. ____________
3. ____________	3. ____________

These graphic organisers help the student determine the location of a country, major geographic features, capital city, area, population etc., Simple charts like this one can be prepared to help learners organise any information.

The funneling effect of environmental degradation can be brought out with this diagram.

Funnel Diagram

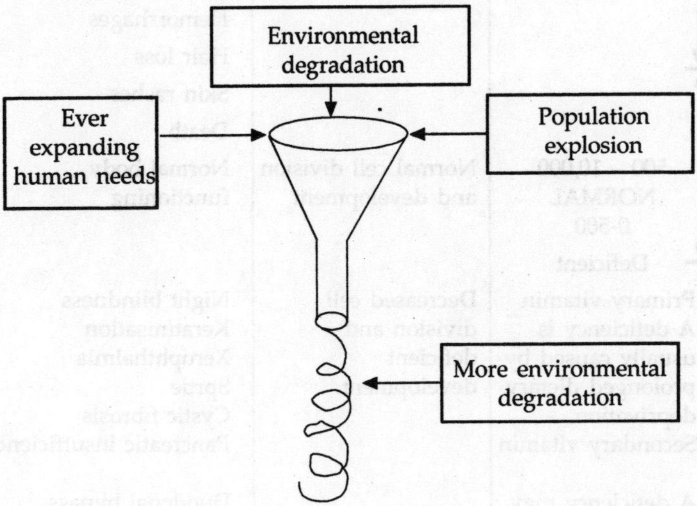

Vitamin A (retinol) is required for the formation of rhodopsin, a photoreceptor pigment in the retina. Vitamin A helps maintain epithelial tissues. Normally, the liver stores 80 to 90% of the body's vitamin A. To use vitamin A, the body releases it into the circulation bound to prealbumin (transthyretin) and retinol-binding protein. -âCarotene and other provitamin carotenoids, contained in green leafy and yellow vegetables and deep- or bright-colored fruits, are converted to vitamin A. Carotenoids are absorbed better from vegetables when they are cooked or homogenized and served with some fats or oils. Vitamin A deficiency and toxicity danger lies both above and below normal range of intakes of Vitamin A. This can be illustrated with the following diagram.

	Effects on cells	*Health Consequences and Etiology*
10,000 and over TOXIC	Over-stimulated cell division	Osteoporosis Liver failure Fractures Birth defects Bone abnormalities Hemorrhages Hair loss Skin rashes Death
500 – 10,000 NORMAL 0-500 Deficient	Normal cell division and development	Normal body functioning
Primary vitamin A deficiency is usually caused by prolonged dietary deprivation Secondary vitamin	Decreased cell division and deficient development.	Night blindness Keratinisation Xerophthalmia Sprue Cystic fibrosis Pancreatic insufficiency
A deficiency may be due to decreased bio-availability of provitamin		Duodenal bypass Chronic diarrhea, Bile duct obstruction Cirrhosis Death

The 'Cascade' effect of Regulation; hunger, appetite, satiation and satiety are depicted here effectively with the help of 'Cascade' diagram on next page.

Another type of diagram that is used to indicate 'depth perception' is illustrated here with an example. A lake is a standing-water and freshwater ecosystem surrounded by land. Standing water ecosystems are characterized by zonation. Deep lakes contain three distinct zones, each with its characteristic communities of organisms – the littoral, limnetic and profundal.

Cascade Diagram

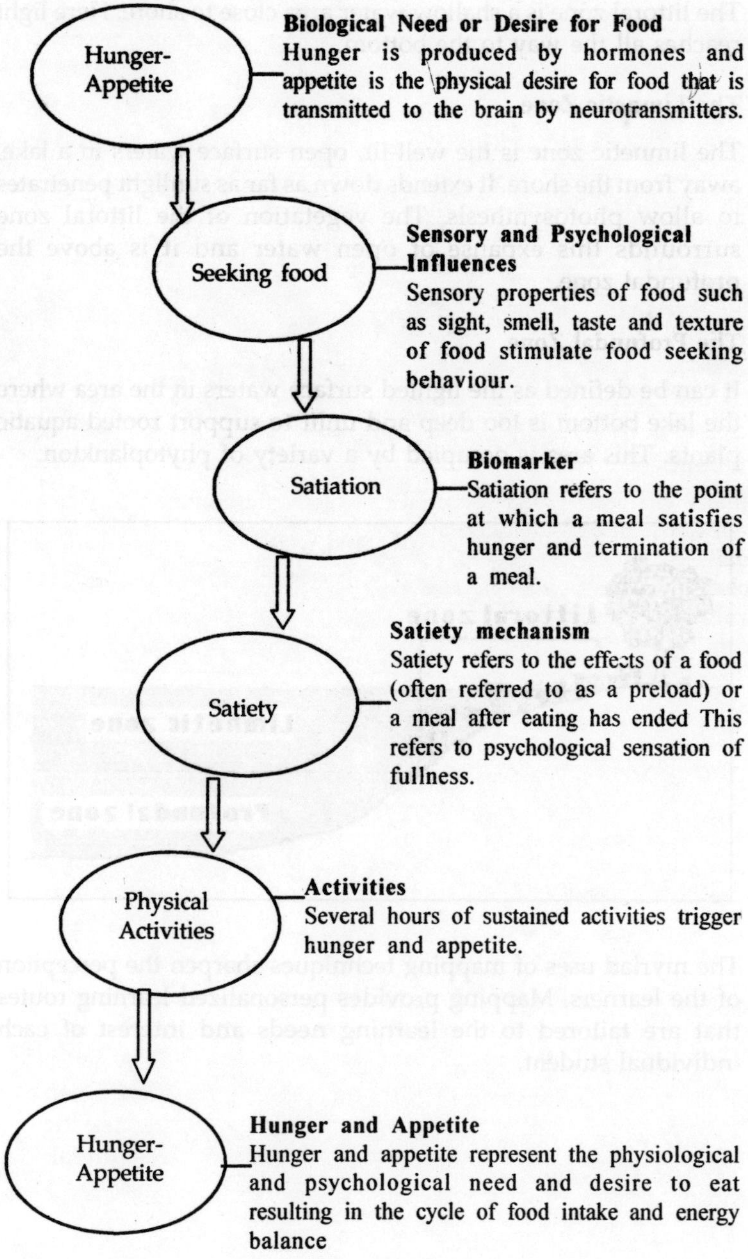

The Littoral zone

The littoral zone is a shallow water area close to shore. Here light reaches all the way to the bottom.

The Limnetic Zone

The limnetic zone is the well-lit, open surface waters in a lake, away from the shore. It extends down as far as sunlight penetrates to allow photosynthesis. The vegetation of the littoral zone surrounds this expanse of open water and it is above the profundal zone.

The Profundal Zone

It can be defined as the lighted surface waters in the area where the lake bottom is too deep and unlit to support rooted aquatic plants. This area is occupied by a variety of phytoplankton.

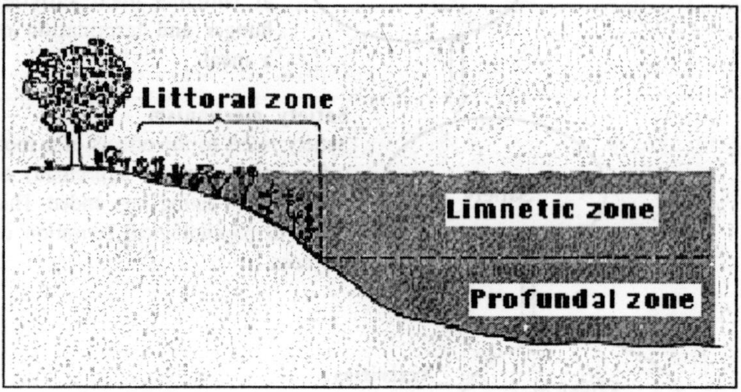

The myriad uses of mapping techniques sharpen the perception of the learners. Mapping provides personalized learning routes that are tailored to the learning needs and interest of each individual student.

16

Mapping Skills for Teaching Concepts in Biology

Chapter Overview

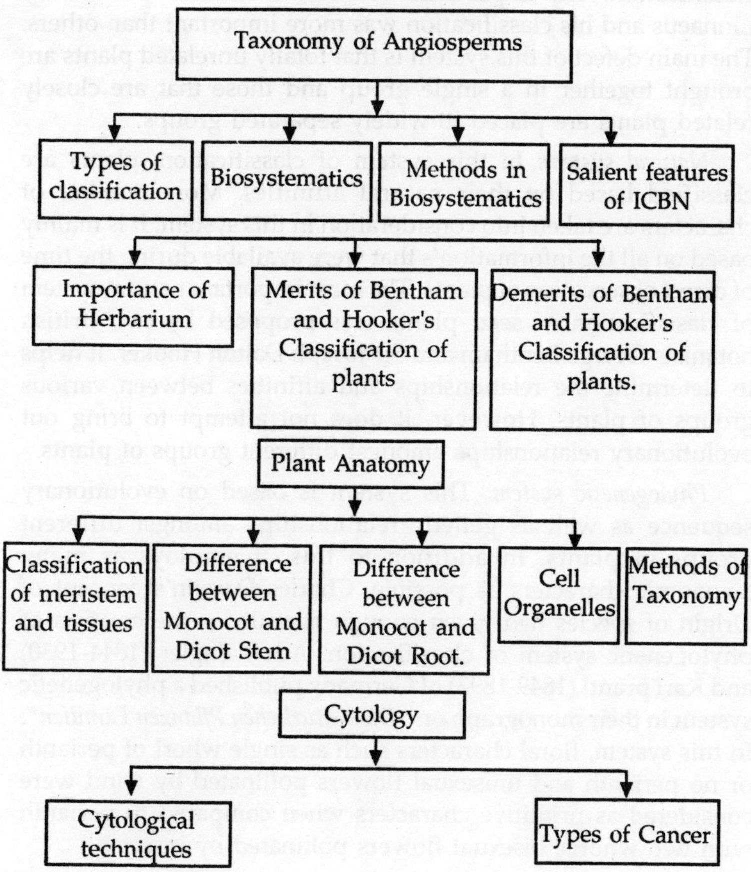

TAXONOMY OF ANGIOSPERMS

Taxonomy is concerned with the laws governing the classification of plants. Taxis means arrangement, nomos refers to laws.

Types of Classification

Artificial system: -It was based on one or at most only a few superficial characters. In 1753, Carolus Linnaeus of Sweden published his book "Species Plantarum" where in he described 7,300 species. He divided the plants into 24 classes based on number, union, length and certain other characters of stamens. Hence this system is also known as sexual system of classification. In those days, it was an important over other systems of classification. The importance of floral characters was felt by Linnaeus and his classification was more important than others. The main defect of this system is that totally unrelated plants are brought together in a single group and those that are closely related plants are placed in widely separated groups.

Natural system: In this system of classification, plants are classified based on their natural affinities. More number of characters are taken into consideration in this system. It is mainly based on all the information's that were available during the time of direct observation of plants. The most important natural system of classification of seed plants was proposed by two British botanists George Bentham and Sir Joseph Dalton Hooker. It helps to determine the relationships and affinities between various groups of plants. However, it does not attempt to bring out evolutionary relationships amongst different groups of plants.

Phylogenetic system: This system is based on evolutionary sequence as well as genetic relationships amongst different groups of plants. In addition to this, it employs as many taxonomic characters as possible. Charles Darwin's concept of Origin of species had given enough stimuli for the creation of phylogenetic system of classification. Adolf Engler (1844-1930) and Karl prantl (1849-1893) of Germany published a phylogenetic system in their monograph on *"Die Naturlichen Pflanzen Familien"*. In this system, floral characters such as single whorl of perianth or no perianth and unisexual flowers pollinated by wind were considered as primitive characters when compared to perianth with two whorls, bisexual flowers pollinated by insects.

1) Network and Comparition Concept Map of Taxonomical Types of Classification

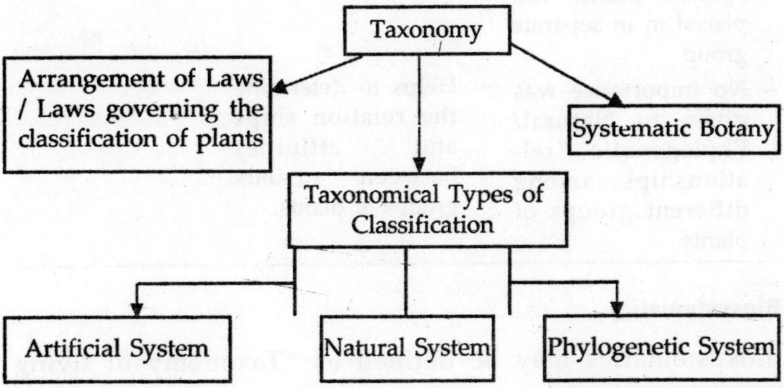

Artificial System	Natural System	Phylogenetic System
– Based on few superficial Characters.	– Based on natural affinities	– Based on evolutionary and genetic relationship amongst different group of plants.
– Carolus Linnaeus published his book "species plantarum"	– More number of characters are taken into considerations	– Darwin's concept of "Origin of species"==> help to produced this system of classification.
– Divided the plants based on number union, length and certain other characters of stamens.	– Mainly Based on Informations available during the observation of plants	– Engler & Karl prantl Die Naturlichen Pflanzen Familien.
– Sexual system of classification	– George Bentham and Dalton Hooker	– According to them, members of Asteraceae of dicotytedons and Orchidaceae of monocotyledons were highly advanced.

– Main defect totally unrelated plants are placed in single group and closely related plants are placed in in separate group	– Does not bring out evolutionary relationships among plants
– No importance was given to Natural/ Phylogenetic relationships among different groups of plants.	– Helps to determine the relation ships and affinities between various groups of plants.

Biosystematics

Biosystematics may be defined as "Taxonomy of living populations".

Aims of biosystematics

Camp and Gily 1943, coined the term 'biosystematics.

i) To delimit the naturally occurring biotic community of plant species.

ii) To recognize the various groups as separate biosystematics categories such as ecospecies, ecotype, cenospecies and comparium.

Methods in the study of biosystematics

Three important methods are as follows,

i) It involves thorough sampling analysis of the taxonomic species under study. Its population, cultivation, geographical range, cytology, anatomy, palynology, phytochemistry, chromosomal number and behavior are keenly observed and studied for finding any genetic differences that may arise among different populations.

ii) It includes determination of ability of different population to interbreed amongst one another to form a variant species with its vigor and fertility. This will reveal the presence or absence of breeding barriers between taxa at various levels.

iii) It involves the study of similarity of chromosomes in the hybrids during meiosis.

Network Concept Map of Biosystematics

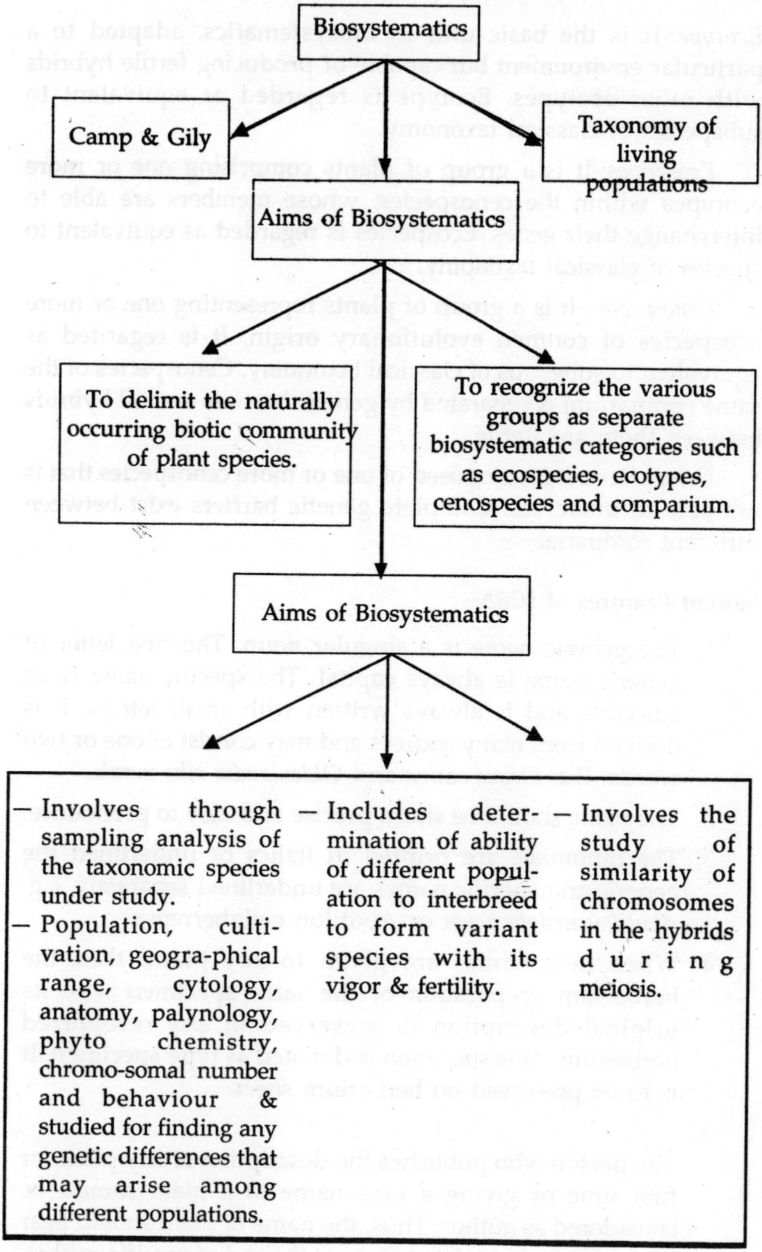

Methods of Biosystematics'

Ecotype:-It is the basic unit in biosystematics, adapted to a particular environment but capable of producing fertile hybrids with other ecotypes. Ecotype is regarded as equivalent to subspecies of classical taxonomy.

Ecospecies:-It is a group of plants comprising one or more ecotypes within the cenospecies, whose members are able to interchange their genes. Ecospecies is regarded as equivalent to species of classical taxonomy.

Cenospecies:-It is a group of plants representing one or more ecospecies of conmen evolutionary origin. It is regarded as equivalent to subg..us of classical taxonomy. Cenospecies of the same comparium is separated by genetic barriers and all hybrids between them are sterile.

Comparium:-It is composed of one or more cenospecies that is not able to intercross. Complete genetic barriers exist between different comparia.

Salient Features of *ICBN*

1. The generic name is a singular noun. The first letter of generic name is always capital. The specific name is an adjective and is always written with small letters. It is derived from many sources and may consist of one or two words. E.g. *Oryza sativa* and *Oldenlandia albo-nervia.*
2. The name should be short, precise and easy to pronounce.
3. The binomials are printed in italics or underlined the generic and specific names are underlined separately. e.g. *Abutilon neilgherrense* or Abutilon neilgherrense
4. When new names are given to any plant, then the herbarium preparation of the same specimen with its original description is preserved in any recognized herbarium. This specimen is denoted as **type specimen.** It is to be preserved on herbarium sheet.
5.

   The person who publishes the description of any plant for first time or giving a new name to a plant should be considered as author. Thus, the name of plant should bear the author's abbreviated name at the end of specific epithet. This is called author citation.

3. Spider Map of Methods of Biosystematics

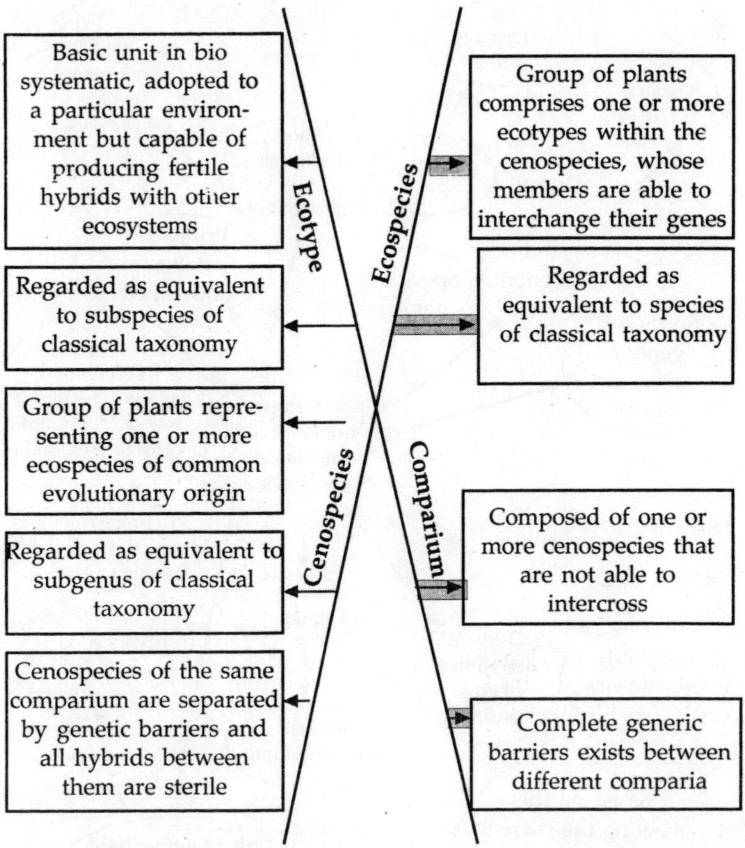

6. The original description of the should accompany the Latin translation.
7. If naming the plant is from a source of error, it is regarded as ambiguous name. It is also called *nomen ambiguun* and is completely ignored from use.
8. If the generic and specific names are the same, it is called tautonym. E.g. *Sassafras sassafras.* Such names are not accepted in the system of nomenclature.

Cluster Concept Map of ICBN

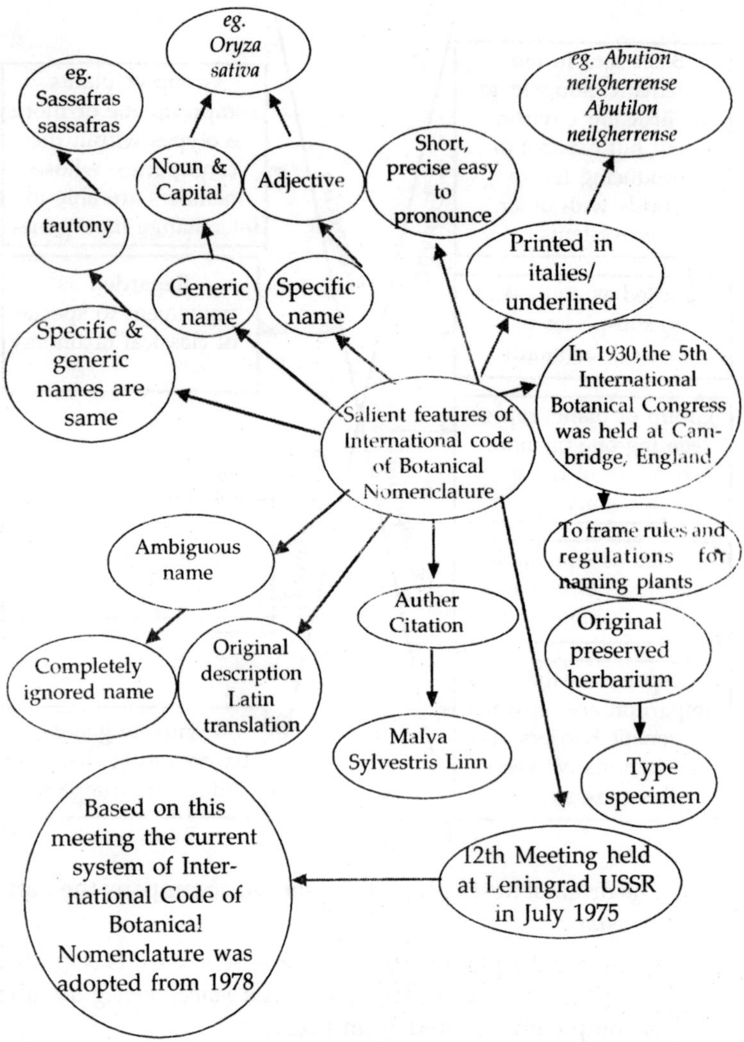

Importance of Herbarium

- Herbarium is a source of knowledge about the flora of a region or a locality or a country.
- It is a data store in which the information on plants or available.

- The type specimens help in the correct identification of plants.
- Herbarium provides materials for taxonomic and anatomical studies.
- Typical pollen characters have been well emphasized in taxonomy. Morphological characters of the pollen remain unaltered even after storage up to nearly 200 years.
- Herbarium is very much useful in the study of cytology, structure of DNA, numerical taxonomy, chemotaxonomy, etc. It acts as a reservoir of gene pool studies.
- Because of its importance, several herbaria have been established at the national and international centers.

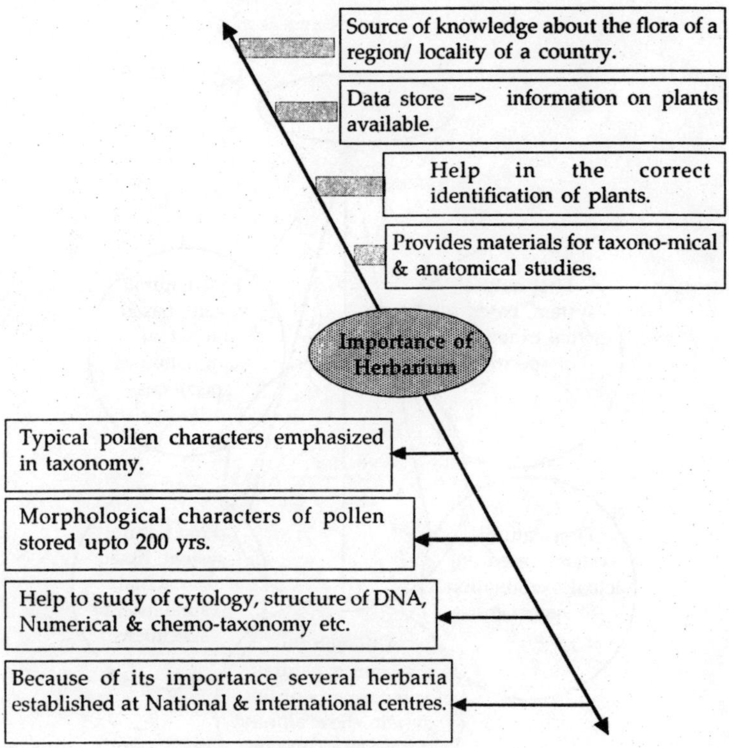

Merits of Bentham and Hooker's Classification of Plants

1. Bentham and Hooker's classification is the first natural system, based on actual examination of specimens.
2. The description of plants is quite accurate and reliable.
3. As it is easy to follow, it is used as a key for the identification of plants in Kew herbarium and several other herbaria of the world.
4. Although this system is natural, some aspects of this system show affinity to modern concepts of evolution.
5. As per Bentham and Hooker's classification of plants monocotyledons are derived from dicotyledons.

Merits of Bentham and Hooker's Classification of Plants

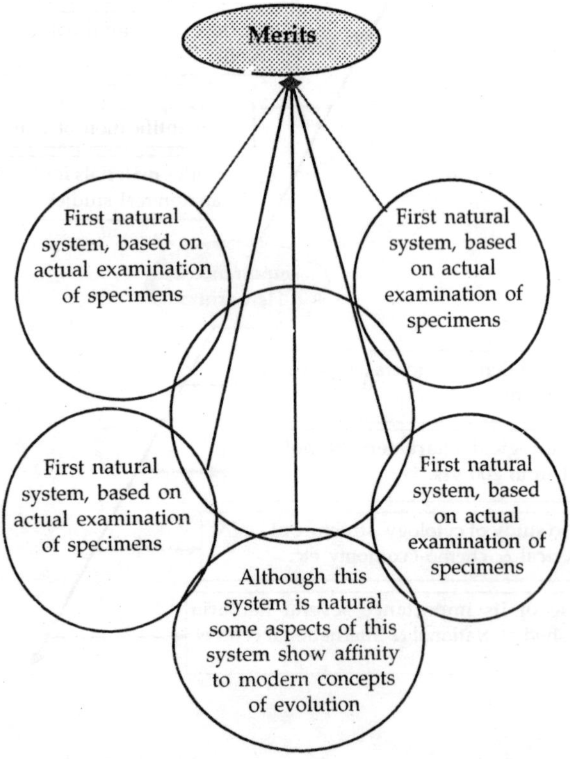

Demerits of Bentham and Hooker's Classification of Plants

1. The placement of gymnospermae in between dicotyledons and monocotyledons is an error, as they are primitive amongst monocotyledons when compared to angiosperms.
2. Several important floral characters have been neglected in this system.
3. Advanced family Orchidaceae has been considered as primitive amongst monocotyledons and it is placed in the beginning of the system.
4. In this system, some closely related families have been separated and placed under different groups.
5. Unrelated families have been grouped nearer.

Demerits of Bentham and Hooker's Classification of Plants

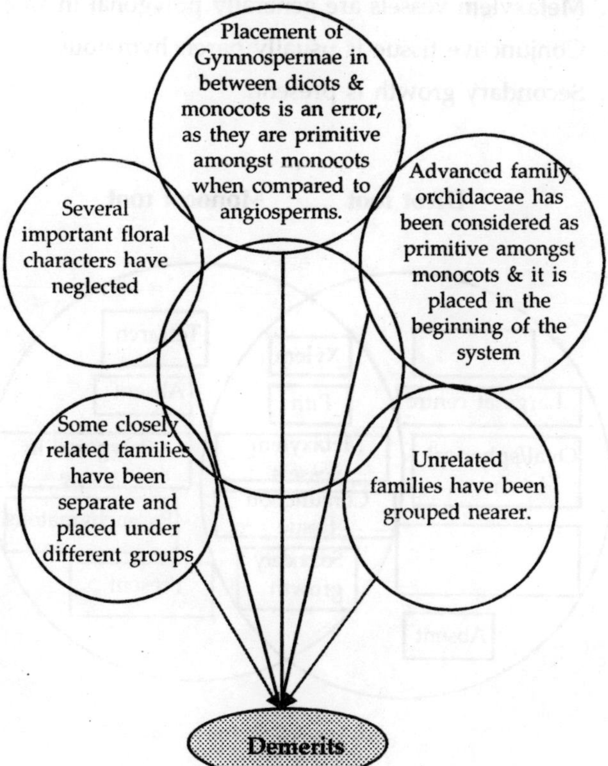

Difference between Monocot and Dicot Root

Monocot root

1. Xylem is polyarch.
2. Pith is usually large at the centre.
3. Metaxylem vessels are generally oval or spherical in shape.
4. Conjunctive tissue is sclerenchymatous in monocot roots like Maize.
5. There is no secondary growth.

Dicot root

1. Xylem is usually tetrarch.
2. Pith is usually absent.
3. Metaxylem vessels are generally polygonal in shape.
4. Conjunctive tissue is usually parenchymatous.
5. Secondary growth is present.

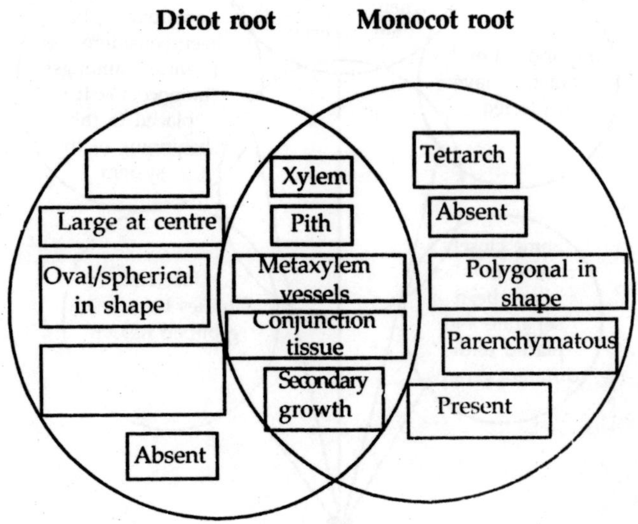

Difference between Monocot and Dicot Stem

Dicot stem

1. Hypodermis is made up of collenchymatous cells.
2. Ground tissue is differentiated into cortex, endodermis, pericycle and pith.
3. Starch sheath is present.
4. Pith is present.
5. Pericycle is present.
6. Medullary rays are present.
7. Vascular bundles are open.
8. Vascular bundles are arranged in a ring.
9. Bundle cap is present.
10. Protoxylem lacuna is absent.
11. Phloem parenchyma is present.

Monocot stem

1. Hypodermis is made up of Sclerenchymatous cells.
2. Ground tissue is not differentiated, but it is a continuous mass of parenchyma.
3. Starch sheath is absent.
4. Pith is absent.
5. Pericycle is absent.
6. Medullary rays are absent.
7. Vascular bundles are closed.
8. Vascular bundles are scattered in the ground tissue.
9. Bundle cap is present.
10. Bundle sheath is present.
11. Phloem parenchyma is absent.

Compare/Contrast Matrix Map of Dicot and Monocot Stem

	Dicot Stem	*Monocot Stem*
Hypodermis	Made up of Collenchymatous Cells.	Sclerenchymatous cell
Ground celltissue	Differentiated into Cortex, endodermis, pericycle & pith	Not differentiated, but it is continuous mass of parenchymatous cell
Starch Sheath, Pith, Pericycle, Medulary rays phloem parenchyma.	Present	Absent
Vascular Bundles	Open and arranged in a ring	Closed & Scattered in the ground tissue
Protoxylem	Absent	Present
Lacuna	Bundle cap is present	Buhdle sheath is present

Plant Anatomy

Plant anatomy (Ana=as under, tamnein=to cut) is the study of internal structure and organization of plants, especially of their parts by means of dissection and microscopic examination.

Tissue and Tissue System

Tissues can be classified into two types-Meristematic tissue and permanent tissue.

Based on its position, the meristem is divided into three types-Apical meristem, intercalary meristem and lateral meristem.

Based on the constituent cells, the permanent tissue is classified into two types-simple permanent tissue and complex permanent tissue.

Simple permanent tissue is further classified into three types-Parenchyma, collenchyma, and sclerenchyma. Parenchyma is classified into aerenchyma, storage parenchyma, palisade parenchyma, stellate parenchyma. Collenchyma is divided into Angular collenchyma, Lacunate collenchyma, lamellar collenchyma. Sclerenchyma is divided into Sclereids and Fibres.

Concept Network Tree of Plant Anatomy

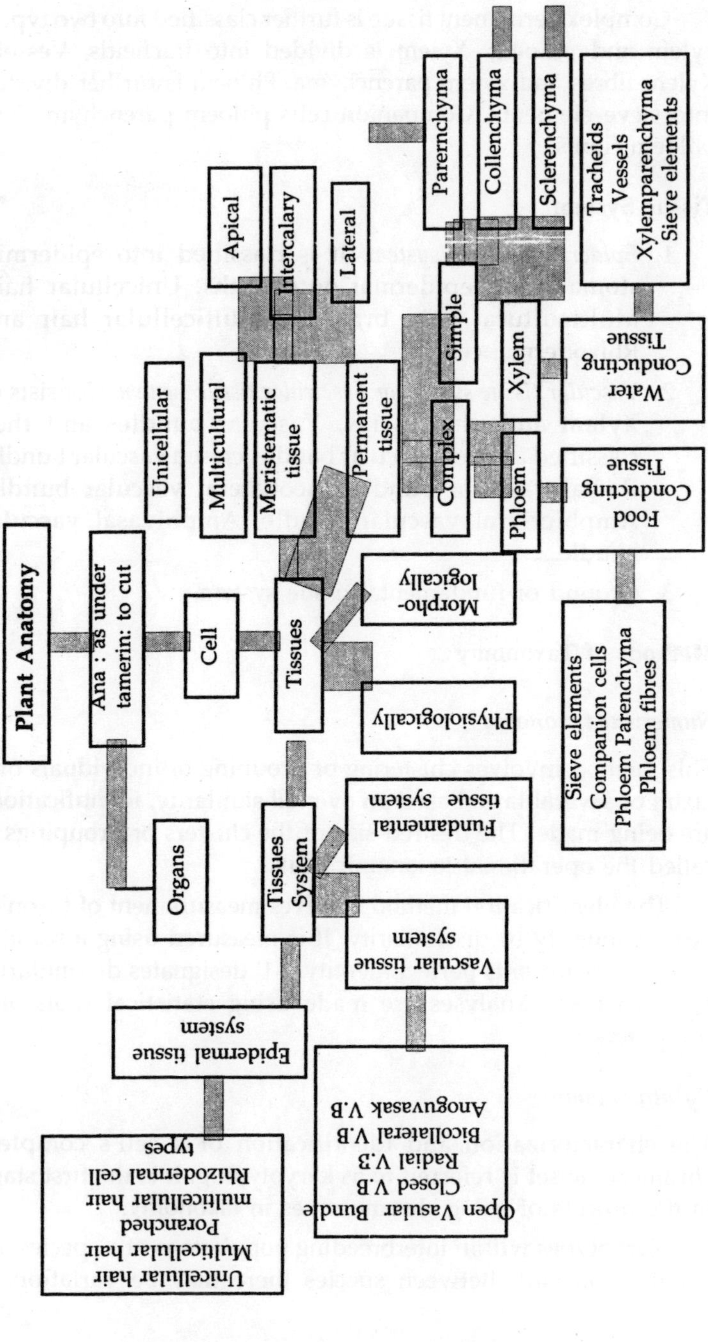

Complex permanent tissue is further classified into two types- xylem and phloem. Xylem is divided into tracheids, Vessels, Xylem fibres and xylem parenchyma. Phloem is further divided into sieve elements, Companion cells phloem parenchyma and phloem fibres.

Tissue System

1. *Epidermal tissue system:* It is classified into epidermis, stomata and epidermal outgrowths. Unicellular hair, Multicultural hair, branched multicellular hair and Rhizodermal cell.
2. *Vascular tissue system or Fascicular tissue system:* Consists of Xylem and phloem i.e., Vascular bundles and they classified as open vascular bundle, closed vascular bundle, Radial vascular bundle, Bicollateral vascular bundle, Amphicribral vascular bundle, Amphivasal vascular bundle.
3. Ground or fundamental tissue system.

Methods of Taxonomy

Numerical taxonomy

This method involves clustering or grouping of individuals of a taxon or several taxa. Based on over all similarity, identifications are being made. The desired size of the clusters or groupings is called the operational taxonomic units.

The identification method involves measurement of taxon to taxon similarity or dissimilarity. It is measured using a scale of 0 to 1. '1' represents perfect identity. '-1' designates dissimilarity between taxa. Analyses are made using statistical tools and computers.

Cytotaxonomy

The characterization and identification of a cell's complete chromosome set is referred to as karyotyping. It is the first stage in the process of using chromosomes in taxonomy.

Karyotypes within interbreeding populations of a species are usually constant. Between species there may be variation in

Comparison Concept Map for Methods of Taxonomy

Methods of Taxonomy

Numerical Taxonomy	Cyto Taxonomy	Chemo Taxonomy	Palaeo Taxonomy
— Method involves clustering/ grouping of individuals of a taxon/ several taxa.	— Characterization and identification of a cells complete chromosome set => karyotyping.	— Refers to the use of information about small molecules produced by action of enzymes.	— Depends on identification and dating of fossils
— Based on overall similarity, identification are being made	— 1st stage in the process of using chromosomes in taxonomy	— Protein fractions in electrophoretic techniques, identification amino acids in chromatography, prevalence of iso enzymes in tissue materials are all tools employed	— Availability of a good complete fossil provides better change for identification
— Desired size of the cultures /groupings => operational taxonomic units	— Karyotypes with in interbreeding population of a species are usually constant	— Occurrence old specific pheromones, colour pigments, toxins also help as keys in taxonomy	— In several fossils, their sections taken through laborious processes have provided the identification features.

(Contd...)

Methods of Taxonomy

Numerical Taxonomy

- Identification method involves measurement of taxon to taxon similarity or dissimilarity
- Measured using a scale of 0-1
  1=> perfect identity
  -1=> dissimilarity between taxa.
- Enormous amount of data are collected for related groups
- Analysis are made using statistical tools & computers.

Cyto Taxonomy

- Between species, their may be variation in chromosome number and size
- Final stage=> chromosomal aberrations as inversion & translocations can give clues regarding intermediary stage.

Chemo Taxonomy

Palaeo Taxonomy

- The fossils are normally studied along with other accompanying fossils, its geographic location and other factors
- Even though it is possible to assign a fossil to a genus or other higher level, fixing the species is not always possible

chromosome number and size. Final stages of chromosomal aberrations such as inversions and translocations can give clues regarding intermediary stages.

Chemotaxonomy

Chemotaxonomy refers to the use of information about small molecules produced by the action of enzymes. Protein fractions in electrophoretic techniques, identification of amino acids in chromatography, prevalence of isoenzymes in tissue materials are all tools employed in chemotaxonomy. The occurrence of specific pheromones, colour pigments, toxins also help as keys in taxonomy.

Cell Organells

S.No	*Cell Organells*	*Discovered by*	*Functions*
1	Cell	Schleiden and Schwann	
2	Cell Theory	Robert Hooke	Basic unit of Organism
3	Protoplasm	Pukinjee	Living part
4	Cytoplasm	Koliker	
5	Plasma membrane	Singer and Nicholson	Limiting layer
6	Endoplasmic	Membrane	Porter Transport of substances in & out
7	Golgi complex	Camillo Golgi	Excretion of waste
8	Mitochondria	Altmann	Power houses
9	Plastids	Schimper and Meyer	Photosynthesis.
10	Centriole	Evan Benidan	Help to cell division.
11	Nucleus	Robert brown	Control unit of the cell.
12	Nucleolus	Fontana	Site for ribosome Production
13	Quantosome	Park and Baggins	Photosynthetic units.
14	Chromosome	Waldayer	Transformation of hereditary Characters.
15	Lysosome	De Duve	Suicidal bags

Palaeotaxonomy

This method depends on identification and dating of fossils. Availability of a good complete fossil provides better change for identification. In several fossils, its geographic location and other factors. Even though it is possible to assign a fossil to a genus or other higher level, fixing the species is not always possible.

Cytological techniques

Cells are transparent and optically homogeneous organizations. They can be observed either directly or after preservation. For direct observation, the specimen needs sufficient contrast. Direct observation is possible by using vital stains.

Vital stains: Vital dyes or stains are taken up by living cells without killing them. They selectively stain intracellular structures without affecting cellular metabolism and function. For example, Janus green B selectively stains mitochondria, Golgi apparatus, nuclear chromatin in a dividing cell can be used to stain yeast cells.

Preserved and stained tissues: For detailed microscopic study, tissues containing cells are passed through various stages. The stages of cell preparation on a glass slide involve killing, fixation and dehydration, embedding, sectioning, staining, and mounting.

Killing and fixation: This process causes sudden death of cells or tissues and preserves freshly killed tissues in as lifelike a condition as possible. A good fixative prevents bacterial decay and autolysis. It will also make different cell components more visible and prepare the cell for staining. The commonly used fixatives are Acetic acid, Formaldehyde, Bouin's solution and Carnoy's fluid.

Dehydration: In this process water vapour are removed from cells or tissues using chemical agents. It is done by using ethanol and benzene.

Embedding: The tissues are infiltrated with molten paraffin wax. It hardens up on cooling and provides enough support to allow thin sections. Very thin sections need to be taken for electron microscopy. Hence plastics are used for embedding.

Sectioning: The embedding material is cut into thin sections of needed thickness. It is done by using an instrument called microtome.

Concept Map of Cell Organells

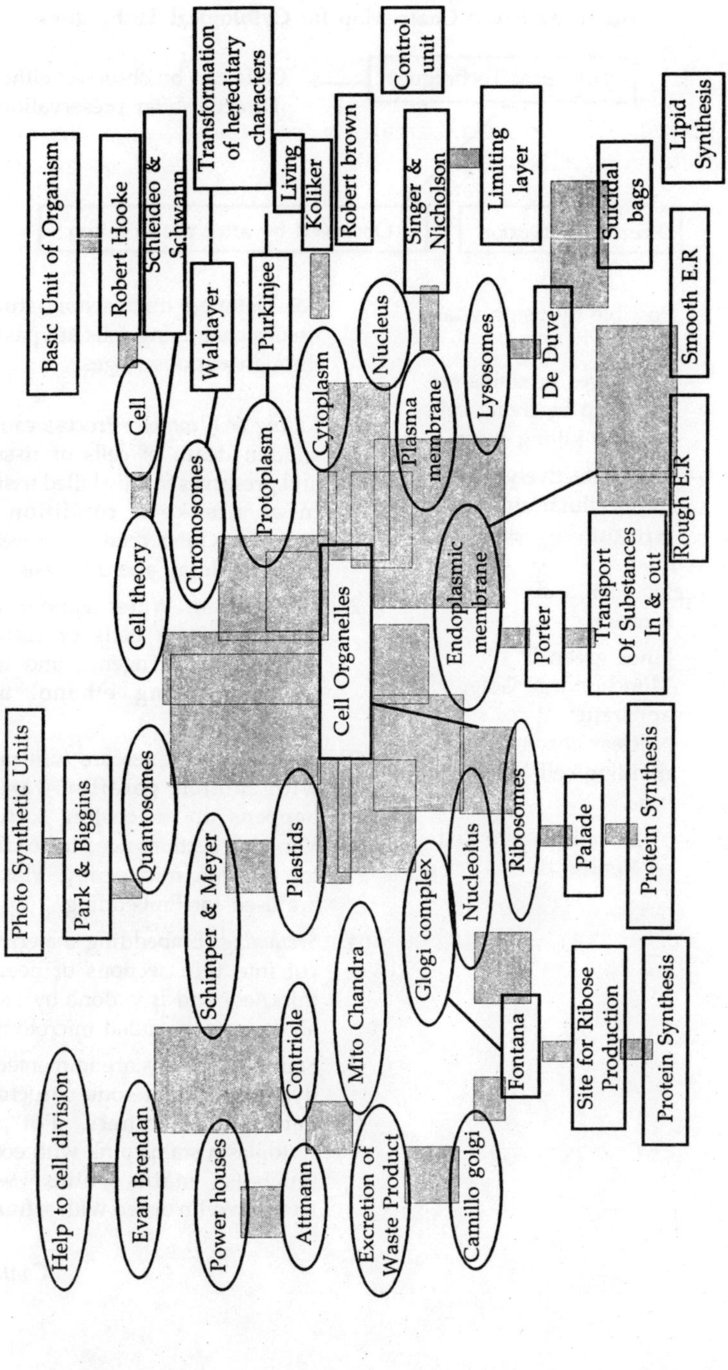

Initiating Event Chain Map for Cytological Techniques

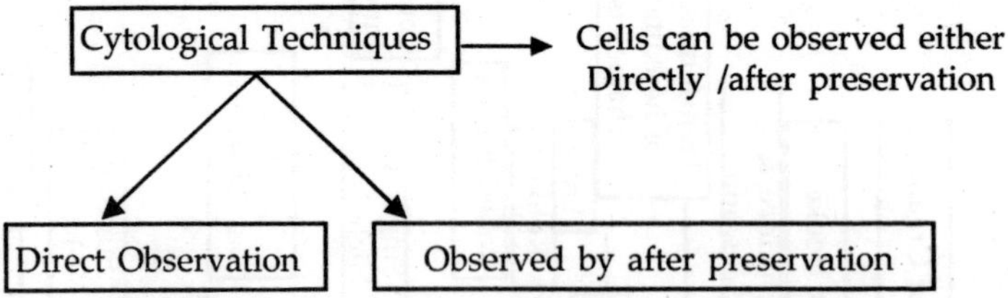

- Possible by using vital stains
- Vital dyes or stains are taken up by living cells without killing them.
- They selectively stain intra-cellular structures without affecting cellular metabolism and function.
- Janus green B Mitochondria, Golgi apparatus.
- Nuclear chromatin in a dividing cell Methylene blue.
- Yeast cells Congo Red or Neutral dye.

For Detailed microscopic study, tissues containing cells are passed through various stages.

1. *Killing & Fixation* : Process causes sudden death of cells or tissues and preserves freshly killed tissues in as lifelike a condition as possible. Good fixative prevents bacterial decay and autolysis.
2. *Dehydration:* Water vapour are removed from cells or tissues using chemical agents, and it is done by using ethanol and benzene.
3. *Embedding:* Tissues are infiltrated with molten paraffin wax. It happens up on cooling section. Very thin sections need to be taken for electron microscopy. Plastics are used for Embedding.
4. *Sectioning:* Embedding material is cut into thin sections of needed thickness and it is done by using an instrument called microtome.
5. *Staining:* Sections are immersed in dyes that stain some structures better than others. For eg. Cytoplasm stains pink with eosin, Nucleus stains blue with haematoxylin or red with safranin.

(Contd...)

(Contd...)

6. *Dehydration:* Stained sections are immessed in ethanol to remove water. The tissue becomes more transparent. It is done gradually by using a series of increasing concentration of ethanol in water. Finally the section is placed in 'absolute' alcohol.
7. *Mounting:* Cleaned sections are mounted on a slide using a sailable medium like Canada balsam. A cover slip is added and the medium is allow to dry.

Cancer Biology

Staining: The sections are immersed in dyes that stain some structures better than others. For example, cytoplasm stains pink with eosin. Nucleus stains blue with haematoxylin or red with safranin.

Dehydration: Stained sections are immersed in ethanol to remove water. The tissue becomes more transparent. Dehydration is done gradually by using a series of increasing concentrations of ethanol in water. Finally the section is placed in 'absolute' alcohol.

Mounting: leaned sections are mounted on a slide using a suitable medium like Canada balsam. A cover slip is added and the medium is allowed to dry.

Cancer is a proliferation of cells which grow in an uncontrolled manner, invading local tissues and spreading widely through the blood or lymphatic to produce secondary deposits or metastases in distant parts of the body. The word 'cancer' comes from Latin, meaning a crab.

Types of cancer: Cancers are named according to the tissues from which they arise.

1) *Sarcoma*—Malignancy in structural tissues. Ex: Osteosarcoma (bones), liposarcoma (fa).

2) *Carcinoma*—Epithelial cancers. Ex: Lung carcinoma, breast carcinoma.
3) *Lymphoma*— Lymphatic tissues.
4) *Leukemia*—White blood cells.(WBC).

Star Map for Types of Cancer

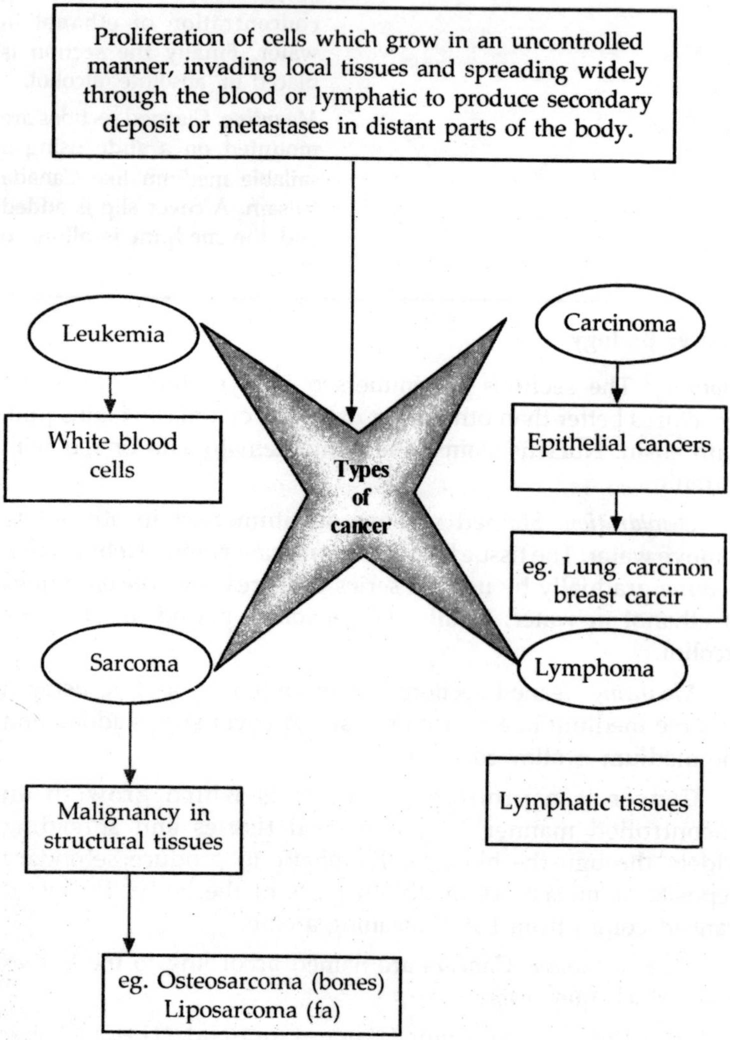

Bibliography

Alvermann, D. E., & Boothby, P. R. (1986)"Children's transfer of graphic organizer instruction", *Reading Psychology,* Vol. 7 No. 2, 87-100.

Anderson-Inman, L., Knox-Quinn, C., & Horney, M. A. (1996)" Computer-based study strategies for students with learning disabilities: Individual differences associated with adoption level", *Journal of Learning Disabilities,* 29(5), 461-484.

Ausubel, D. (1963) *The Psychology of Meaningful Verbal Learning,* New York: Grune & Stratton.

Ausubel, D. (1978) "In defense of advance organizers: A reply to the critics", *Review of Educational Research,* 48, 251-257.

Ausubel, D., Novak, J., & Hanesian, H. (1978) *Educational Psychology: A Cognitive View* (2nd Ed.), New York: Holt, Rinehart & Winston.

Beck, Isabel L., Omanson, Richard C., and McKeown, Margaret G. (1982) "An Instructional Redesign of Reading Lessons: Effects on Comprehension.", *Reading Research Quarterly,* vol. 17, no. 4, pp 462-481.

Boss, Candace A., Anders, Patricia L., Filip, Dorothy, and Jaffe, Lynne E. (1985) "Semantic Feature Analysis and Long-Term Learning." in *Issues in Literacy: A Research Perspective,* edited by Jerome A. Niles and Rosary V. Lalik, Rochester, New York: National Reading Conference, pp. 42-47.

Boyle, J. R., & Weishaar, M. (1997) "The effects of expert-generated versus student- generated cognitive organizers on the reading comprehension of students with learning disabilities", *Learning Disabilities Research & Practice,* 12(4), 228-235.

Bulgren, J., Schumaker, J. B., & Deschler, D. D. (1988) "Effectiveness of a concept teaching routine in enhancing the performance of LD students in secondary-level mainstream classes", *Learning Disability Quarterly,* 11(1), 3-17.

Buzan, T. & Buzan, B. (2000) *The Concept Map Book* (London, BBC Worldwide Ltd).

Carnes, E. R., Lindbeck, J. S., & Griffin, C. F. (1987)"Effects of group size and advance organizers on learning parameters when using microcomputer tutorials in kinematics", *Journal of Research in Science Teaching,* 24(9), 781-789.

Clements-Davis, G. L., & Ley, T. C. (1991) "Thematic preorganizers and the reading comprehension of tenth-grade world literature students". *Reading Research & Instruction,* 31(1), 43-53.

Darch, C. B., Carnine, D. W., & Kammeenui, E. J. (1986) "The role of graphic organizers and social structure in content area instruction", *Journal of Reading Behavior,* 18(4), 275-295.

Davis, Zephaniah T., and McPherson, Michael. D (1989) "Story Map Instruction: A Road Map for Reading Comprehension", *The Reading Teacher,* December 1989; 232-240.

Dewey, John. (1938) *Experience and Education,* NY: Collier Macmillan.

Downs, R.M. and Stea, D. (1973) *Cognitive Maps and Spatial Behavior: Process and products*In Image and Environment Downs, R.M. and Stea, D. (Eds.) Chicago: Aldine (1973:8-26)

Enright, D. Scott, and McCloskey, Mary Lou. (1988) *Integrating English: Developing English Language and Literacy in the Multicultural Classroom,* Reading, MA: Addison-Wesley.

Fawcett, Gay. "Graphic Organizers.", *Ohio Middle School Journal,* FalllWinter 1991; 18

Flood, James L., and Lapp, Diane (1988) "Conceptual mapping strategies for understanding information texts." , *The Reading Teacher,* April 1988; 780-783.

Flood, James L., Jensen, Julie M., Lapp, Diane, and Squire, James, R. (1991) *Handbook of Research on Teaching the English Language Arts,* NY: Macmillan, 1991; 617.

Gallego, M. A., Duran, G. Z., & Scanlon, D. J. (1989) "Interactive teaching and learning: Facilitating learning disabled students' transition from novice to expert", *Literacy Theory and Research,* 311-319.

Gardill, M. C., & Jitendra, A. K. (1999) "Advanced story map instruction: Effects on the reading comprehension of students with learning disabilities", *The Journal of Special Education,* 33(1), 2-17.

Golledge, R. G., Rivizzigno, V. L., & Spector, A. (1974). *Analytical methods for recovering cognitive information about a city.* Paper presented at the IGU Regional Conference, Palmerston North, New Zealand.

Golledge, R. G., Rivizzigno, V. L., & Spector, A. (1974). An experimental design for recovering cognitive information about a city. In R. G. Golledge (Ed.), *On Determining Cognitive Configurations of a City: Vol. I—Problem Statement, Experimental Design and Preliminary Findings* (pp. 135-204): NSF Grant #GS -37969.

Hagen, Joan E. (1980) "The Effects of Selected Prereading Vocabulary Building Activities on Literal Comprehension, Vocabulary Understanding, and Attitudes of Fourth and Fif~h Grade Students With Reading Problems", Madison, WI: *Dissertation Abstracts International*, 1980.

Heimlich, Joan E., and PiKelman, Susan D.(1986) *Semantic Mapping: Classroom Applications,* Newark, DE: International Reading Association.

Herl, H. E., O'Neil, H. F. Jr., Chung, G. K. W. K. & Schacter, J. (1999) "Reliability and validity of a computer-based knowledge mapping system to measure content understanding" *Computers in Human Behavior*, 15(3-4), 315-333.

Hudson, P., Lignugaris-Kraft, B., & Miller, T. ( ) "Using content enhancements to improve the performance of adolescents with learning disabilities in content classes", *Learning Disabilities Research & Practice*, 8 (2), 106-126.

Idol, L., & Croll, V. J. (1987) "Story-mapping training as a means of improving reading comprehension", *Learning Disability Quarterly*, 10(3), 214-229.

Merkley, D.M. & Jefferies, D. (2001) "Guidelines for implementing a graphic organizer", *The Reading Teacher*, 54 (4) 350-357.

Moore, D.W., & Readence, J. E. (1984) "A quantitative and qualitative review of graphic organizer research", *Journal of Educational Research*, 78(1), 11-17.

NCREL, 1988 Ruzic, R. & O'Connell, K., (2001). *An overview: enhancements literature review.*

Newby, R. F., Caldwell, J., & Recht, D. R. (1989) "Improving the reading comprehension of children with dysphonetic and dyseidetic dyslexia using story grammar", *Journal of Learning Disabilities*, 22(6), 373-380.

Novak, J. D. (1990) "Concept maps and Vee diagrams: two metacognitive tools to facilitate meaningful learning", *Instructional Science*, 19(1), 29-52.

Piaget, Jean. (1979) *"Correspondences and Transformations." (DiLisio, Trans.)* In *The Impact of Piagetian Theory on Education, Philosophy, Psychiatry, and Psychology,* edited by Frank B. Murray, Baltimore, MD: University Park Press, 1979.

Quirk and Greenbaum (1973) *A University Grammar of English,* Longman Group Limited pp. 148-151).

Rivizzigno, V.L. (1976) & Golledge, R. G. (1974) A method for recovering cognitive information about a city. In B. Honikman (Ed.), *EDRA 5 Proceedings, Vol. XI* (pp. 9-17). Milwaukee, WI: Environmental Design Research Association, Inc.

Scanlon, D., Deshler, D. D., & Schumaker, J. B. (1996) "Can a strategy be taught and learned in secondary inclusive classrooms?", *Learning Disabilities Research & Practice*, 11(1), 41-57.

Sinatra, R. C., Stahl-Gemake, J., & Berg, D. N. (1984) "Improving reading comprehension of disabled readers through semantic mapping", *Reading Teacher*, 38(1), 22-29.

Smith, Nila Banton.(1964) "Patterns of writing in different subject areas", *Journal of Reading*, October 1964; 31-37.

Stahl, Steven, and Vancil, Sandra J.(1986) "Discussion Is What Makes Semantic Maps Work in Vocabulary Instruction." *The Reading Teacher*, October 1986; 62-67.

Tindal, G., Nolet, V., Blake, G. (1992). Focus on teaching and learning in content classes. Resource Consultant Training Program, University of Oregon Eugene; Training Module No. 3, 34-38.

Tolman, E. C. (1948) 'Cognitive Maps in Rats and Men', *The Psychological Review, 55(4)*, 189-208.

Toms-Bronowski. *An Investigation of the Effectiveness of Selected Vocabulary Teaching Strategies With ~ntermediate Grade Level Children*. Madison, WI: Dissertation Abstracts International, 1983.

Vacca, Jo Anne L., Vacca, Richard T., and Gove, Maly K. (1991) *Reading and Learning to Read: 2nd ed. NY:* HarperCollins.

Vacca, Richard T., and Vacca, Jo Anne L. (1986) *Content Area Reading*, Boston, MA: Little, Brown, 1986.

Vygotsky, L.S. (1978). *Mind and society: The development of higher mental processes*. Cambridge, MA: Harvard University Press

Willerman, M., & Mac Harg, R. A. (1991) "The concept map as an advance organizer", *Journal of Research in Science Teaching*, 28(8), 705-712.

The Mind Map Book

How to Use Radiant Thinking to Maximize

Your Brain's Untapped Potential

Published by Penguin Group/Dutton 1993

ISBN 0-525-93904-0

Edward C. Tolman. Retrieved Mar. 28, 2005, from www.a2zpsychology .com Web site:

http://www.a2zpsychology.com/great psychologists/ edward c tolman.htm.

http://en.wikipedia.org/wiki/Programmed_instruction"_Category: Educational psychology

Grammar Myths Debunked
http://www.wikipedia.org

Index